ROSALIND RUSSELL is a jo[illegible] two decades of international exp[illegible] as a foreign correspondent for Reuters and *The Independent* in East Africa, the Middle East and Asia. Her reporting included the fall of the Taliban in Afghanistan, the war in Iraq and Myanmar's Saffron Revolution. Her first book, *Burma's Spring*, published in 2014, was described by *Asian Affairs* as "reportage at its best" and reached number one in the UK Kindle non-fiction bestseller list. She lives in London with her husband and two daughters, and currently works for the *Evening Standard*.

Praise for *The End of Where We Begin*

"Engages our hearts with vivid and moving stories…written with extraordinary clarity, compassion and impact"
Moore Prize 2021 Jury

"A beautiful, moving and important book about survival and the power of the human spirit"
Simon Reeve, broadcaster and author

"Insightful and deeply humane. With vivid detail, it captures the essence of life in South Sudan at a particularly turbulent moment in its history"
Michela Wrong, author of *Do Not Disturb* and *It's Our Turn to Eat*

"A powerful and authentic account"
Luka Biong, author of *The Struggle for South Sudan*

"A captivating…compelling chronicle of the refugee experience of displacement, loss and hope"
Ka'edi Africa

"Powerful and moving…stays in your memory long after you have put it back on your bookshelf"
Publishing Post

"A harrowing and intimate account of civil war's toll"
Kirkus Reviews

THE END OF WHERE WE BEGIN

Rosalind Russell

Published by Eye Books
29A Barrow Street
Much Wenlock
Shropshire
TF13 6EN

www.eye-books.com

First edition published by Impress Books, November 2020

Cover design by Nell Wood
Typeset in Adobe Caslon Pro and Brother 1816 Printed

British Library Cataloguing in Publication Data
A catalogue record for this book is available from the British Library

ISBN 9781785633713

Printed and bound by CPI Group (UK) Ltd, Croydon, CR0 4YY

For Ruby and Mattie

'There is no story that is not true'
Chinua Achebe
Things Fall Apart

Author's Note

In April 2023, news bulletins were briefly dominated by the eruption of civil war in Sudan and the race to evacuate foreign nationals from the city of Khartoum, which overnight became a lethal battleground between the army and a mutinous militia group. But once Western nations had airlifted their citizens to safety, the gaze of the world's media quickly moved on, even with millions of Sudanese civilians uprooted and on the move.

The same scenario had played out with painful similarity a few years earlier, when convulsions of violence ripped through the capital of Sudan's neighbour South Sudan, forcing hundreds of thousands of people to flee. I was working as a journalist in London on human rights stories, filing reports of the sudden and dramatic exodus. Civilians were streaming across the border into Uganda on a scale not seen since the Rwandan genocide of 1994. Over the following months, Bidi Bidi refugee camp in Uganda, a city of sticks and tarpaulin, grew to become the largest in the world, home to a quarter of a million people. Aside from the occasional article here and there, however, the scale of the crisis and its terrible human consequences were barely touched upon in the media.

This was a region I knew from my years as a correspondent for Reuters in East Africa when I reported from South Sudan on its struggle for independence. My life was settled and my daughters were still in primary school, but I felt the pull of my old life as a foreign correspondent; I wanted to return to the region to document the stories behind these astonishing numbers.

I first arrived in Bidi Bidi in February 2018 on the back of a motorbike driven by a Ugandan mental health counsellor, James. He worked for a small charity that struggled to pay for the fuel needed to run their battered four-by-four vehicle around the five zones of the sprawling camp. Bidi Bidi, in the north-western corner of Uganda, covered a hundred square miles and took two hours to traverse along dirt roads and rutted tracks. Its low hills were dotted with tarp-roofed shelters, newly built mudbrick homes, acacia and neem trees.

Only registered refugees were allowed to stay overnight in the camp – or settlement, as it was known, as it had no fences or boundaries. The camp commander signed and stamped my clearance letter to visit in daytime. I stayed in a guest house in the small trading town of Yumbe, which was booming following the arrival of hundreds of mostly Ugandan aid workers recruited to help in the crisis. The aid agencies War Child, Save the Children, the International Rescue Committee, World Vision and TPO helped me with transport and access, allowing me to spend several weeks in Bidi Bidi and later Rhino Camp and Nyumanzi settlement. The Franciscan Brothers kindly hosted me at Adraa Agricultural College in Nebbi where South Sudanese refugees had been enrolled on short courses.

All the people in this book and the events they describe are real. The main three characters – Veronica, Daniel and Lilian – asked me to use their own names, but I have changed the names of some family members and others to maintain the confidentiality of those who were unable to give their consent. The stories are drawn from extended in-person interviews conducted in 2018 and 2019 in northern Uganda and South Sudan and, after that, from many conversations by phone, WhatsApp, Facebook messenger and email. Daniel and Lilian spoke to me in fluent English. In interviews with Veronica I at first relied on Save the Children staff, or her neighbour Wilbur to translate from her native Arabic. But when I met her alone I discovered her English was really quite good and we were able to talk without an awkward male presence.

With introductions from aid workers and officials who supported me in the camp, I interviewed more than fifty refugees over several months and heard many stories, often heroic and heart-breaking, which have been hard to leave out of this book. The characters who form the heart of the narrative stood out, as not only did they have remarkable stories to tell, but they were keen to tell them. They were willing to accept me into their homes, allowed me to follow their daily routines and patiently answered my endless questions. This means they are perhaps not a representative sample, but I am confident that their lives, while extraordinary, were typical in the context of the camp. Similar tales of loss, courage, compassion and ambition were repeated over and over. Important, harrowing detail was often relayed in a brutally matter-of-fact manner or quickly skipped over as it was considered so mundane. The lives I have explored in the pages that follow are snapshots of a far wider refugee experience.

These are not my stories. Despite some authorial interventions to provide political background and context, I have chosen to remain absent from the narrative and I have tried to write closely from the protagonists' perspectives. I have attempted as far as possible to replicate the inner thoughts of my characters as they described them to me. I do not know what goes on inside their heads but I have tried to construct a realistic narrative from their descriptions of their journeys, conversations, emotions and life events. The intimacy of some of the accounts reflects the startling openness and generosity of Veronica, Daniel, Lilian, Asha and others during our conversations. It's hard to overestimate their courage and generosity in speaking to me. While all the dialogue in the book comes from their own descriptions and accounts, I have sometimes used literary licence to reconstruct experiences or interactions and I have also had to alter the chronology of some personal events in order to give the narrative shape and momentum.

I documented the experiences of the refugees with written notes, audio recordings and photos and video. In the course of my reporting I also spoke to aid workers, community volunteers, teachers, health workers, religious leaders, government officials and UNHCR representatives. I was helped with fact-checking by Christine Wani, a journalist and South Sudanese refugee living in Bidi Bidi. I visited the South Sudanese capital Juba in October 2018 to research the events described in the book and better understand the environment from which the refugees fled, where I was assisted by the Reuters correspondent Denis Dumo. I have also relied on news articles, human rights reports, publications by academics and researchers and books about South Sudan's civil war.

The title *The End of Where We Begin* is derived from a Dinka blessing to the Earth. In the context of this book, however, it illustrates the injustice of young lives brutally interrupted by war. While the rightful expectations of these three young people have been snatched away, I hope that in illuminating their search for meaning and opportunity amid extremes of violence and exile I challenge the often stereotyped narrative of refugees. The following pages explore the consequences of civil war in a fragile African nation, but although specific to a time and place, I hope the stories of Veronica, Daniel and Lilian resonate beyond the confines of the refugee camp where I met them.

There is a boy in the camp who always walks around with his head tilted to the left side. It looks uncomfortable, as if it is seized up in that position. The boy is young, but old enough to look after himself. He never goes to school; mostly, he sits under the mural of the dancing children and the dove of peace in the dusty, disused playground, next to the water tap. He likes to watch the women filling up their containers. Their infants, strapped to their backs, sometimes start crying because the boy looks so weird. It's tempting to try to straighten him up, maybe massage his neck and shoulders, relieve the tension. Just looking at him makes everyone feel tense. When anyone asks him why his head is askew like that – they rarely do – he answers calmly and politely. To him, his explanation makes perfect sense.

In South Sudan, he hid in a tree when the soldiers came. He lay flat on a good, strong branch, quite high up among the leaves, and made his breathing go quiet. It was hard for him to stay quiet when he watched the soldiers slaughter his family – his grandmother, mother, father, older brother and younger sister – but he managed. He listened in silence to the screams of his loved ones and the soldiers' shouts and laughter. He clung to the tree all night. He kept still for hours, even when he had to relieve himself. He didn't sleep. He had to be sure the soldiers had gone.

In the morning, he climbed down. When he reached the ground, his legs buckled under him, they felt prickly and numb. He stumbled over to his mother's body and lay down beside her, face to face in the dirt. Her eyes were open and staring. He waved away the flies and stroked her cheek and hair. She still wore the delicate string of coloured beads around her neck. It was getting hot but she was cool; he had never felt a person like that. He stayed there for a while, he might even have dozed off, but when the sky darkened above him, he bolted up. Birds were swooping down, flapping their great wings for balance. They were big, ugly birds and they started to peck at a wound in his big brother's flank. The young boy let out a scream. He jumped up and with flailing arms ran at the vultures, stumbling over the bodies of his family. The birds took off, squawking, their wings fanning the warm, putrid air. They circled above. The boy ran into the house to look for blankets or sacks to cover the bodies. But the soldiers had upturned their home; everything was gone. He ran to the cassava field to see if the spade was in its hiding place, halfway up the third furrow. It was there.

As the sun blistered down, the boy dug a grave for his family. At first, he kept running back to the bodies to shoo away the birds, but he could not do both. He dug and dug, his body dizzy, the sound of his panting in his ears. He must have fainted, because he opened his eyes to find himself lying in the grave. It still wasn't deep enough; he had to keep going. Shovel, throw, shovel, throw. The soil was red and dry. Sweat trickled into his mouth. The sun plagued him all day, dipping and cooling only when he had dug a hole big enough to fit five bodies. Well, he hoped it was big enough; he had never dug a grave before.

He went back to where the bodies lay. It had started to get dark. The boy's eyes were wide and alert, but he didn't see the mutilated corpses in front of him, because that would have killed him too. He saw his family: his grandmother, his mother, his father, his sister, his brother. With them, he had spent fourteen perfect years on this earth. He liked to say this, when he got to the camp, if people asked.

Now he is committing them back to the earth. He begins with his grandmother, the lightest. He kneels down beside her, unsure of how to pick her up. He turns her on to her back. He sees her gentle, weathered face. He turns her back on to her front. He needs to get some purchase. He burrows his right shoulder down under her waist, reaches under her body to her right arm, clutches it, and tries to stand. His skinny legs wobble like a newborn calf's. He adjusts his grandmother's body on his shoulder and brings his left arm behind his neck to steady the load. He staggers with her across the family homestead to the new family grave. He returns four more times. It is dark when he covers the bodies with the soil.

"I carried them on this side," he tells people in the camp, patting his right shoulder; his head crooked awkwardly to the left. "They were many and they were heavy. That's why I can't put my head straight now." He is usually smiling, but his eyes are blank. "Sometimes I hear them calling for me. They want me to come back. They are too squashed in."

The boy pats down the fresh grave with the back of his spade and lays down on top, sprawled like a starfish. He listens to the throb of the crickets and the soft wind in the leaves. It is peaceful. He wants to close his eyes and fall asleep. But also, he wants to live.

He hauls himself up and starts to run.

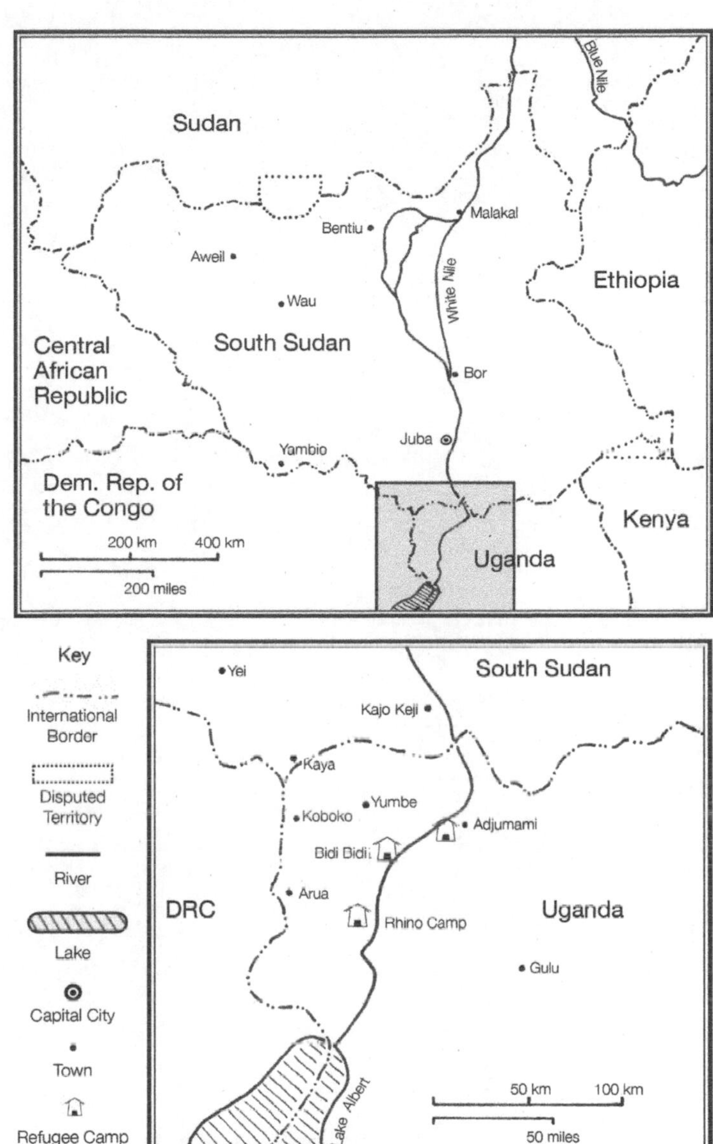

Map of South Sudan and Northern Uganda

PROLOGUE

With the first hint of dawn the camp begins to stir. The darkness fades and the small, twittering birds that share this desolate, unsatisfactory home with a quarter of a million refugees launch into their feeble chorus. A pale, violet light seeps through the cracks around the door to Lilian's one-roomed home and slowly her eyelids open. Another day. She sits up on the narrow iron bedstead, plants her feet on the dirt floor and steps straight outside in her nightdress. The jumbled remnants of a dream slip away as her muscle memory walks her, barefoot, to the water tap.

Things move slowly in the camp. Time and money, the twin engines of life elsewhere, aren't so important here. There are hardly any jobs and very little cash. It is always hot, so no one rushes, but there are still certain chores that need to be done. At the water pump, neat lines of yellow plastic jerrycans radiate from the single tap like sun rays in a child's drawing. Lilian sets down her container at the end of a row. Dozens of women have got there before her. The tap won't be switched on until seven, and they have scratched their initials onto the containers so they can come back to claim their places once they've got the cooking fires going.

Lilian lives by herself in the camp, but she hasn't always been alone. She was married at nineteen and she and her husband had a beautiful baby boy. In South Sudan she had a job she loved and a vegetable garden where she grew cassava, maize, groundnuts and beans. Now, six years on, she has lost her husband, her son, her house and her land. She could blame the war for that, but actually she blames herself. This is an issue she needs to work on, her counsellor has told her.

She walks back home with her friend Asha. The two young women, tall and lean, stroll towards the rising sun, responding to its nurturing warmth like flowers, standing straighter, tilting up their chins. Lilian feels wonder that she can do this, live another day, go on. She doesn't understand why she is still alive, why she fetches water, sweeps, cooks and talks to her neighbours. But something is driving her forward.

"So, are you serving today?" Lilian asks her friend.

Asha is a quiet, industrious woman. She has started her own business in the camp selling her home-brewed maize liquor; she half-starved herself to get the seed money but now it's paying modest dividends, for which she thanks God because she has just found out she has a baby on the way.

"Yes, but I only have two bottles left. I'm closing before counselling starts," Asha says.

"Those men will be disappointed!" says Lilian, talking

about the drinkers who assemble under the tree as the sun starts to get hot. Asha serves them her powerful, fermented brew in plastic mugs and they talk and laugh and fight and usually fall asleep, half propped up on the knots of the tree roots. Asha wakes them when it's dark and sends them home. "How about," suggests Lilian, "after we've finished today, I'll help you with the next batch."

Asha smiles at her friend. It's rare to see Lilian in such good spirits. They set down the water drums next to the beaten metal doors of their adjacent mud-brick homes and Asha hears Lilian softly humming as she starts to prepare the porridge that must sustain her until tomorrow.

Today is counselling day and, although they would never say so, they are both looking forward to it.

Daniel is sitting on the bench he has made, leaning back against the warm clay of the shady side of the house. He is idly strumming his guitar, more from habit than enjoyment; he knows that no one really wants to hear him play. He watches his mother and sister. They are squatting next to two basins of water. His mother is washing their clothes with a bar of laundry soap, handing the items to Tabitha, his sister, who rinses and wrings and hangs each piece up on the line. Daniel watches the woodsmoke drift up and cling to the wet clothes; everything will smell worse than when they started, he thinks, but says nothing. He admires them, he really does.

He can't believe he's here, back in a refugee camp. He feels safe again, but that is the only positive. He and his sister grew up in another camp, in Kenya – that was when they thought their father was dead. It was only when he reappeared and they started a new life in South Sudan did Daniel realise what life in a refugee camp had meant: rules, restriction and, worst of all, stagnation. Some people like it, the boundaries and the certainty, but Daniel isn't one of them.

He has an appointment today, such a rare occurrence he must be careful not to forget to go. There is so little to punctuate their lives, it's easy to lose track of the days. He'd love to have a calendar, like the one they used to have with pictures of a happy family drinking Ovaltine. The father in a work suit, a smiling mother and two healthy children, a boy and a girl, both smart in their school uniforms. They looked so clean and happy. Daniel's family had kept it for years afterwards, turning it back to January at the start of each year and going through the months again just to see the pictures, the days were all wrong. But anyway, his appointment, his next session of counselling, is definitely today, Tuesday, two days after Sunday which is the only day that's different in the camp. That's the day they go to the open-air church with the tree log pews and his mother tries to get her hands on some cabbage or onions to distract from the monotony of their food rations.

A couple of months ago Daniel was given a questionnaire from one of the aid organisations. They were worried about the refugees, because of all that they'd been through. They wanted to help everyone, especially the ones who had seen the worst of it, to stop them from going mad. Daniel filled in the questionnaire and he really enjoyed it; no one had ever made such enquiries about his well-being, his sleep patterns, his health and his feelings before. Some of the things they asked he had never even considered. He'd never been encouraged to dwell on his emotions, or even acknowledge them, so holding that biro and going through the whole survey was a real novelty, and in some ways, a relief.

It was tempting to skew the answers. He thought he knew what they were looking for, what would get him onto the treatment programme, but he tried to be completely honest. Some of the questions made him think about things he had never thought of before, or made him feel upset.

Did he sleep badly, were his nights full of terrors? Yes. If it wasn't the fighting in Bor it was often the bus crash and the faces of his school friends. Did he isolate himself from others? He hadn't thought about it like that, but on consideration, yes. Was he emotionally short-tempered? His mother would say so. Was he depressed? He didn't know what that meant. Did he suffer from headaches? Body aches? Yes, but that was from the accident. Did he ever feel suicidal? That question just made him feel guilty, unworthy. Only people who had really suffered badly could think of something like that. What he'd been through was just the same as everyone else.

Veronica is wearing her stripy top. It has wide brown, orange and white stripes. It's actually a child's top, but it's made of stretchy material. The sleeves reach just past her elbows and the curve of her belly shows above the waistband of her skirt but it still looks good. Veronica looks good in anything. She is long-limbed and graceful, her skin luminous, her head shaved, her face perfection. Veronica is the seventeen-year-old mother of two-year-old Sunday, who has come with her to the group counselling session. The little girl wears a grubby ivory-coloured nylon party dress – a cast-off from another child in another world. She loves the dress, but the material makes her skin itchy when it's hot.

The sun is burning through the white canopy of the tent's roof – sheets of white UNHCR tarpaulin stitched together. Veronica, the youngest in the counselling group, is sitting on a plastic mat and the other women are clucking around her. They are kind, she thinks, she doesn't feel judged, like she usually does.

"Sunday! Sunday!" they call, delighted by the round-cheeked toddler who runs around the circle of women sitting on the floor. There are two men in the group too; they are standing, waiting for the session to start. The little girl stumbles and falls, carefully picks herself up from the bare floor, checks her dirty palms and sets off again.

"So, when are you expecting the next one?" asks the woman sitting next to Veronica. Although Veronica hasn't told anyone about her pregnancy, her slender frame means it's impossible to hide. What she really wants is to go back to school, but she's not sure how that will work, with Sunday and the new baby. She fiddles with the silver crucifix that her father gave her at her Confirmation when she was eleven years old. That seems a long time ago now.

"In May," Veronica, almost whispers in her soft, dreamy voice. "It will be raining by then."

To her relief, further enquiries are curtailed by James the counsellor who claps his hands to get the session underway. They all look up. Each one of them, for their own reasons, is keen for this to work. He claps out a rhythm, which Veronica and the others duly repeat. It's to wake them up, help them concentrate, he says, pacing around their circle, exuding his usual enthusiasm. This is session eight of the programme and today, he tells them, they will continue to share their most difficult experiences with each other – but only if they want to, of course.

A faint line forms between Veronica's eyebrows. She's not sure if she has the confidence to speak today. She struggles in this kind of environment. Sensing the change in atmosphere, Sunday toddles back to her mother and plants herself on her lap. Veronica puts her arms around her daughter and dips her head so the little girl's soft cheek rests against hers.

Lilian, the woman who always wears a yellow dress, passes around sheets of paper. They are handouts from James, to help them understand their feelings. Lilian likes to look for these jobs to do, Veronica has noticed. Last week, Lilian told the group how she lost her little boy when she ran from South Sudan. They had been caught in a battle, and everyone had been separated. She has no idea if he is dead or alive. Although Veronica has her own problems, she felt the aching emptiness of this woman's grief. She cried when she heard that story.

"Can you two share one?" asks Lilian, licking the end of her finger and separating a white A4 sheet from the pile. She smiles at Sunday, who is now sitting quietly in her mother's lap, examining her fingers. Veronica thanks her and accepts the piece of paper, watching Lilian's smile drop as she moves on round the circle.

PART 1

CHAPTER 1

Veronica

2012

It was after her father died that Veronica got into bad ways. She had been a few months off twelve, with two younger brothers and a little sister. She had always thought she looked like a boy, like her brothers Santino and Simon. She had wanted to grow her hair, to have braids like some of her friends, but they were too poor for hairstyles, her head was always shaved. Now, more than a year later, she looked less like a boy. Her bones ached from the growing she had done; her hips were too wide for her old school skirt and she had had to dip her head to get through the low door to their dingy house. In class, she noticed her teacher's eyes fall on her small breasts; she hated that, and she hated the painful stomach cramps and the shame of her monthly bleeding.

Her father had been a soldier, but he was off duty when he was killed. It was a robbery, on the road outside Bentiu, the town where they lived. That's where they found his body. He was part of the liberation struggle and had been a rebel fighter in the Sudan People's Liberation Army all of his adult life. But he never got to see the prize for which he'd fought for so long: he died in early 2011, just a few months before South Sudan finally won its independence.

Her mother hadn't coped. With no earnings from their father, the family ate stewed okra every day, and every day with less salt. Veronica's little sister Amani cried each evening, lying on the bed they shared. Their mother was a soldier too. She had met Veronica's father in SPLA ranks and stayed on after the peace was signed, working as a cook. But her income was a pittance, and even with the goat bones and vegetable scraps she sometimes brought home from the barracks, the family was hungry.

At home, Veronica spoke less and less. At school, with her friends, she was okay, she didn't discuss her father, the situation at home, or anything like that. Her friends didn't talk about their own domestic problems either. At break, the girls still enjoyed their skipping songs, or they sprawled under the big tree, scribbling in their exercise books and talking about silly things; it was a place where they were happy. On the evening her mother told her they would leave and go to Juba to look for money, food, a job, Veronica said nothing. She walked out of their thatched-roofed *tukul*, grabbed an empty jerrycan and marched to the well, trying to recall her father's voice. She let her tears fall down her cheeks. The neighbour's children stood and stared.

"Veronica! Wait!" The boy was calling her. "Wait! Why do you always walk so fast?"

They were in front of the classroom with windows of wire mesh that let in the traffic dust, the fumes and the constant noise of the unfamiliar city. Juba wasn't much for a national capital, but to Veronica it was overwhelming. In Bentiu she rarely saw a face she didn't know; here everyone was a stranger. Men with reeking breath and yellow eyes leered at her on her way to school. In the market she was swindled by the water-seller and felt so ashamed she let herself go thirsty for a week. Their new home was a tin-roofed shack that their mother padlocked them into every night. At school she was behind in all subjects. The girls giggled at her heavy Arabic tongue, made faces behind her back and decided not to be her friend. The boys had mostly ignored her, except for this one. His name was Jackson.

"Will you be at church on Sunday?" he enquired. Veronica didn't look at him, but she could feel the heat of his attention. She fixed her gaze on his ankles exposed by his too-short navy school trousers. His shoes were old black slip-ons, a cast off from an older brother, or a second-hand purchase from the market.

"Yes, as usual," she replied sharply, switching to Arabic to answer the question posed in English. English was the language of instruction in the Juba schoolroom and one of the many things that made Veronica feel like an outsider in this city. She was too shy to speak it; it felt alien on her tongue.

"Good," said Jackson, switching back to English. He leaned forward, but not too close. Veronica still refused to look at him. "I'll see you there."

Veronica had no idea why Jackson was interested in her. Her beauty was something she had yet to fully understand. People had told her she had inherited her mother's looks, her smooth forehead, almond eyes with a silver waterline and her wide, transforming smile. In Bentiu, Veronica's uncle had once remarked that she would be worth at least ten cows. Jackson was tall and lanky. He smelled sweet; he didn't have that stale odour of the other unwashed boys. He was Nuer, like her, and Catholic too; he wore a small silver Virgin Mary pendant around his neck on a leather cord. He was fourteen, a smart kid, already in Primary Five. Veronica knew there were plenty of other girls at school who might be flattered to be singled out by Jackson, but to her, the attention was excruciating.

Even her poorest friends – the ones who would sometimes go days without eating and slept on the wet ground in the rainy season – had some sort of Sunday-best clothes. Veronica's own church outfit – a white blouse, a short, candy-pink jacket and matching skirt with a thin plastic belt – had been the same for two years. The zip on the skirt was now a struggle to fasten and the hem was too high. She had some black court shoes with worn heels that her aunty had passed on and the silver cross that her father had bought for her Confirmation, when her whole family had sat at the front of the church. They had never been rich, but looking back, things had been easier then.

The Mass started at seven thirty in the morning, but it was acceptable to come later and the cavernous St Joseph's in Juba took more than an hour to fill up. By the start of the main sermon, ushers wearing white tabards had to escort late arrivals down the aisles and ask those already seated to scoot up on the crowded wooden pews until thigh was firmly pressed against thigh. Veronica was squashed between her brother Santino and a large lady to her right who was fervently mouthing passages from her Bible, even as the purple-robed priest addressed the congregation, reminding them of the parable of the talents, exhorting them to use their God-given gifts in the service of the Lord. Heat and sweat built between their adjoining limbs as the service reached a noisy, happy crescendo. The choir sang songs praising Jesus, the words projected onto the screen above the altar so they could all join in. Apart from a scratchy radio blaring in the market, the only music Veronica heard was through the booming PA system at church, and this was one of the reasons she looked forward to Sundays. She was beguiled by the harmonies of the choir, the soft-rock solos of the guitarist and the soothing promises of deliverance from her family's earthly challenges. She would sway to the Gospel beat, pricks of sweat forming on her nose, and lose herself in the message of love and hope. She always left church with a feeling of being scrubbed clean and a resolution to be a better child of God that week, more virtuous and devout.

She walked down the steps to the gravelly area under the bell-tower where the congregation mingled and chatted as the sun grew uncomfortably hot on their heads. She clutched her little black Bible and the silky drawstring bag with the pearl embroidery that she always carried to church, but which contained nothing. She stood close to her mother, holding her little sister's hand. Veronica looked like she was listening politely to her mother's cousin, also a migrant from the north, but her cheeks were burning and she was finding it hard to concentrate on the woman's complaints. To her left, just in her sightline beyond another group of churchgoers, was Jackson, smart in his suit. He was staring straight at her.

It was partly her loneliness, partly his persistence that eventually sealed their friendship. He was the first male confidant she had ever had, and proved to be a good listener, especially when, after a few months, she was able to talk to him about her father. She talked about what had happened for the very first time, because her father's murder was never mentioned at home; his absence was only referred to in the context of their straitened circumstances.

Jackson, two years ahead at school, also started to help her with her homework. Veronica struggled with the basics of writing and arithmetic. The sudden move to Juba had given her a fevered head, she told Jackson, and everything she had known from school had slipped away. She had failed to move up from P3 to P4 last year, and if she failed the end-of-year examination again, she would find herself in the same class as her younger brother.

"So, what is a fraction?" Jackson asked in his gentle, serious teaching voice.

"A fraction is a quantity that is not a whole number," Veronica replied, confident when asked to parrot a phrase often repeated by her teacher.

"And different fractions can have the same value, is that correct?" he probed.

She scanned his eyes for the right answer.

"Yes," she guessed.

"Good. So now you can place these fractions in order."

The numbers he had carefully written out in pencil on the spare pages of a used exercise book swam before her eyes: two over three, one over four, four over six.

They were lying flat on their bellies, propped up on their elbows on the rubber mats of the after-school club, their heads together but their bodies at a right angle – any closer and they would attract the attention of the adult monitor. They were wearing their white school shirts, he with his tatty trousers and she with her thick, pleated skirt. Veronica waggled her heels distractedly in the stuffy heat. This was the only place they could meet and relax in Juba, a "child-friendly space". There had been nothing like it in Bentiu, but aid agencies had piled into Juba since independence, each with an idea of how to help war-shattered South Sudan to its feet. The aim of the centre was to give children a protected area away from school to play and socialise, to help their rehabilitation. At thirteen, Veronica didn't know this. Later she would become more expert in the lexicon of aid and disaster – she would learn about food distribution points, shelter kits and nutrition centres. For now, she was grateful for the breeze-block building, its walls painted with colourful murals, for the paper and pens that were sometimes provided, the quizzes and the games, and spending time with Jackson.

She wriggled her hips to move up the mat and get a bit closer to the book, so her head was right over it, the numbers right under her face, but it didn't seem to help.

"I know," said Jackson, "I have a big, juicy mango. I can cut it into three and give you one piece or cut it into four and give you two pieces – which one do you want?"

"But that's easy!" Veronica smiled. Everything was easier with Jackson.

CHAPTER 2

Daniel

December 2013

Daniel always felt like someone in South Sudan. It was because of his father, of course. At boarding school in Uganda he was popular enough, but his unusual height, gappy front teeth and weird accent marked him out as an outsider. On the juddering bus ride home for Christmas, he sat alone by the window and watched the gentle curves and green tobacco fields of Arua county give way to a harsher landscape of rocky scrub dotted with desert trees as they drove towards the border. A bag of charcoal was jammed against his thigh; he was penned in, ignored. He dutifully performed the task of slamming shut the sliding window when an oncoming vehicle was sighted, to keep out the gritty red dust that flew up from its wheels, then opening it again when the air had cleared. No one acknowledged his efforts. At the border post, after presenting his new, eagle-crested South Sudanese passport and some obligatory crumpled notes of 'tea money', he was directed through with nods, grunts and total disinterest. But when he emerged on the South Sudan side there was William, his father's driver, waiting next to a purring white Land Cruiser that would transport him along the highway to his father's home in Juba in air-conditioned comfort.

It would be a quiet Christmas. Only sixteen-year-old Daniel had been summoned back to the house where his father lived with his fourth wife and their young son. Daniel's mother and his sister Tabitha had stayed behind in Uganda. His mother had tried to stay on good terms with her much younger successor. When she saw Daniel onto the bus she had pressed a pot of honey into his hands – he was to give it to his stepmother, a gift from the third wife to the fourth. "Remember your prayers," she had instructed him. "Make me proud."

His father was a giant of a man with flappy ears. He had been an SPLA fighter, rising through the ranks to field commander. When Daniel was a toddler, his father went missing while on mission. The family presumed he was dead and lived for years in a refugee camp in the north of Kenya until one day he resurfaced and brought them back home without explanation. Daniel was ten and had no memory of him. When he saw him again the first thing he noticed were his ears – big, sticky-out ears like his own.

The ex-guerrilla fighter was now a colonel in the national army of the new South Sudan and a senior official in the defence ministry. His house, close to the military barracks at Giyada, was an apricot-coloured bungalow with a green tin roof, a flushing toilet and a shiny, tiled floor throughout. Daniel liked to lounge on the couch and watch TV, revelling in a break from the strict routines and chores of school. Although it was nearly Christmas, his father was busy, as Daniel had expected. The colonel had swapped his gun and shortwave radio for a desk and laptop – he was doing important work, helping to build the world's youngest country.

Independence from Sudan's government in Khartoum two years earlier had come after decades of war and starvation that had ravaged the south. On nearly all measures of development and prosperity, South Sudan came last. At independence, the country had just a few miles of paved roads; it was littered with landmines and an adolescent girl was more likely to die in childbirth than finish school. Its first leaders, President Salva Kiir and his deputy, Riek Machar, had been bush commanders like Daniel's father. Now these former rebels were tasked with making the transition from liberation struggle to government, entrusted with building a functioning state from the ashes of war. It was a colossal task, and although the colonel hadn't said so, things were not running smoothly.

For Sunday morning breakfast, Daniel's stepmother had laid the white tablecloth on the dining table and prepared millet porridge, hard-boiled eggs, papaya slices and black tea. Daniel sat next to his half-brother, little Akuei, who shared the name that his father gave to all of his wives' firstborn sons. The boy would change into his suit for church after he had finished his breakfast; Daniel wore a stiff collared shirt of his father's and ate with care.

He usually avoided discussing serious matters with his father. He knew so little, and his father was impatient of ignorance. At school in Uganda, Daniel had been oblivious to political manoeuvrings back home, but now, between watching Nigerian juju dramas and premiership football, he had been catching up on the news from SSTV.

Simmering tribal hostility between the Dinka and the Nuer had bubbled up again. Salva and Riek had fallen out and the new government was fracturing along ethnic lines. Daniel had thought independence would bring peace, but now South Sudan's new leaders were fighting among themselves. The rift between Salva, from the dominant Dinka group, and his now ex-deputy Riek, a Nuer, had dominated the headlines. A few days earlier, Riek, who everyone knew regarded himself as a more fitting leader of South Sudan, had accused the president of dictatorial tendencies and warned that the fledgling nation was heading towards an abyss. On Saturday night, just a couple of days after Daniel had arrived, the news anchor announced that Salva had summoned his rival to a meeting at the presidential palace the following day.

"So, what will Salva say to Riek?" Daniel ventured over breakfast. "Do you think he'll take him back?"

"You mean our president, Daniel," his father frowned. "He will do what is best. We may think we have differences but we are all brothers. We fought together for our nation. Now we must fight for peace," he said solemnly, wiping his mouth and rising from the table.

"It's time for us to go and pray."

He left the room. He seemed annoyed and Daniel wished he'd kept quiet.

At about nine o'clock that night Daniel heard a pop, then another, then another. Slowly at first, then one, by one, by one. It started to speed up – *pop, pop, pop* – until a barrage of gunfire was coming from the nearby barracks. His stepmother rushed from the bedroom where she had dozed off as she soothed her young son to sleep. His father had been out since church that morning. One of the guards who manned the gate burst into the house, just as the phone started to ring. It was Daniel's father.

"It's Riek's people. They are starting," his father said, his voice sharp. "His people will fight for him. Stay there. Turn off the lights. Stay inside, I'll be back later."

Briefings from the presidential palace would later report that the Sunday meeting had not gone well. Riek had arrived with a list of demands that Salva refused to entertain. There could be no concessions and no place for him in the government until he proved his absolute loyalty, the president had said. Witnesses in the room, heavy with grand, lacquered wooden furniture, later reported that Riek had said nothing, rose from his chair and walked out, flanked by his two bodyguards. There was no joint press conference for the journalists who had gathered outside, and no written communiqué. The statements came later, when the first shots were fired. A fight between Dinka and Nuer soldiers within the presidential guard quickly escalated; soldiers split along ethnic lines and battles spread quickly across the city.

Daniel and his stepmother turned off all the lights, but

a white glare still lit up the windows from the outside. The solar! The panels on the roof powered all the outside lights in the compound. Daniel sent the guard to climb up and disconnect the power source. A few minutes later they plunged into darkness. The clatter of gun battles became louder and more urgent; a percussion boom of tank-fire sent a shudder through the house, followed, minutes later, by a sulphurous waft of explosives through the mosquito screen. He heard the sound of shattering glass followed by shouting and a woman's scream. His stepmother hurried to the bedroom to sit with her son. Daniel sat alone in the living room.

He was worried, of course, but being in his father's house gave him a sense of invincibility. A battle was raging, and not too far away, but surely they wouldn't touch the colonel's house. How could they? He was far too important. It wasn't until his father returned at eight in the morning, his bloodshot eyes betraying a hint of panic, that Daniel fully grasped the danger they were in.

"Juba is split in two," his father told them in the kitchen, speaking fast. Daniel had last seen him in his Sunday suit. Now he was dressed in camouflage fatigues, an eagle and star on his epaulettes, his sleeves rolled up.

"Riek has taken his men from the barracks, they have their weapons. They're digging in now. They'll start again. I need to get you all out, to Bor. I have a vehicle here. Daniel, you will take the family."

Daniel knew his father well enough not to question his instructions. He dashed to his bedroom and packed a few things in his small backpack, his phone included.

His stepmother squatted down to help her son put on his sandals. In a matter of minutes they were squashed into the cab of the military pickup parked in the drive. His father shut the door and banged twice on the car roof to see them on their way. The driver would take them over the bridge to the industrial area where they would find another car to take them to safety in his family's hometown, Bor, a hundred miles down the White Nile.

CHAPTER 3

Veronica

December 2013

"We never see you here!" Veronica's mother scolded her. "I need more help with the water, and with the cooking. You come home and expect to eat but it is *you* who should be serving *us*!"

"Yes, Mummy," Veronica replied without protest, squatting down to sift the bits of husk from the basin of pale, dried maize. She worked fast, stopping only to stoke the fire and set some water on to boil.

Her brothers Santino and Simon observed the exchange without comment. They were used to their mother's criticism of their sister, of her failure to step up to her role as eldest daughter, to pull her weight. Veronica was fourteen now; she should be running the household, her mother had complained, she was more than old enough to fetch water and firewood, do the washing, cook and sweep out the house.

Her mother had a job to do and Veronica finished school by four. *What did she get up to*?

Veronica would respond to these dressings-down by jumping on her tasks with vigour. She tipped cow peas into the simmering water, refilled the water container and started on the boys' laundry, wringing out water red with dust from their shorts. She never demurred; she didn't want a fight. The boys knew why. After more than a year in Juba, Veronica didn't go to the child-friendly space after school any more. Her name was still on the list on the wall; last year she had been elected to the student committee that met each month to discuss events like the talent show and poetry competition, or the occasional workshops on adolescent health or HIV. But Veronica missed the committee meetings these days. She had stopped going sometime in the rainy season.

After school, as the students filed out of the gate, the boys had watched their sister subtly detach herself from her classmates and hover in the shade of the school sign, waiting for Jackson. When he showed up, he would excuse himself from his group with a fist bump or wink, and the young couple, barely acknowledging each other and certainly never touching, would head off to the main road, in the direction of Gudele, towards Jackson's house.

It was the same every day. Afterwards, Veronica would rush home late. Santino, who wasn't being trained up for womanly duties, would usually get the fire going at least. Even her little sister would help by filling up the two small jerrycans. If not, they'd be eating in darkness. Veronica was grateful and would try to repay her siblings for their discretion regarding her absences. She would put a little more food on their plates, which meant less on hers, and let them go first with the water in the bucket shower, which meant just a dribble for her. She didn't care about those things really. She was happy.

In the Christmas holidays, Veronica's mother made sure she gave her elder daughter a long list of chores to keep her occupied. While her brothers were allowed to go and play football, Veronica, with Amani as her assistant, had to get up before dawn to start the fire in the little brick kitchen outside their shack. She would sweep the dirt ground in front of the door, a never-ending task that gritted her eyes and needed repeating several times a day if their small plot was to look well presented. She would prepare the porridge. After breakfast she would wash up, taking care to use the minimum of water, which they had to buy at the market and which had started to swallow up nearly a third of her mother's measly earnings. On weekdays, Veronica and her sister would head to the market to buy some sorghum flour, a few onions, sometimes beans, chickpeas and a couple of tomatoes. The stallholders, weather-worn ladies sitting cross-legged under sun umbrellas in front of carefully arranged piles of red onions, calloused lemons or basins of pulses and grains, would remark on Veronica's beauty and tease her about marriage. Veronica was more at ease with her body now, walking with her chin tilted up and a slight sway in her hips. But she could never get used to the lascivious looks she got from the men – many older than her father – repairing bikes or selling home-brewed *marissa*.

On Sunday, after the family had been to church and her

mother had gone to work, Veronica returned to the house, took down the washing and prepared supper on the embers of the fire. She washed, changed and waited – when the boys came home from football she would slip away for the evening. Her schoolwork was still a struggle and there were examinations in January. Jackson was helping her to study – all perfectly true, she assured herself.

By six o'clock she was with him. In Bentiu, she had had several good friends, girls she had known since she was a baby, whom she had grown up with and had loved like sisters. They had always been close and honest with each other. But in Juba, she had made no real friends among the girls. Jackson was her one friend, as well as her boyfriend and her tutor. He lived with his aunt and uncle in Gudele, a messy district of hand-built shacks set along dirt tracks under the dramatic rocky outcrop of Jebel Kujur. Since his uncle had started working away, and his aunt spent all day at her stall cooking chapatis, Veronica and Jackson could meet in privacy.

They stepped inside and it took a moment for their eyes to adjust to the gloom. It was ten days to Christmas, and the two-roomed house was decorated with pieces of golden tinsel and two plastic reindeer that hung on the wall with bright red noses that used to light up. The young couple didn't say a word. Sex between the teenage lovers was instinctive and never discussed before or after. There was no protection; both had been beneficiaries of sexual health workshops run by NGOs, but somehow they didn't see the information they were offered as applying to them. Both regarded themselves as God-fearing Catholics, and they fully understood that fornication was a sin. So it was easier not to acknowledge what they were doing, let alone discuss the potential consequences.

An hour later and they were sitting, as usual, under the kerosene lamp that hung from the tree outside the house when Jackson's aunt returned with warm chapatis for them to share. Veronica, in a pleated fuchsia pink skirt that reached down to her calves, was struggling with some English spellings that she needed to learn: *visualise, finalise, capitalise, economise, equalise.* She wrote them out in lines, over and over in her slow, careful print. She found it easier to learn them by rote than to associate any meaning to the long list of words she never used. Jackson was doing his own revision – he was in his last year of primary and was desperate to move up to the senior grades. Mathematics in P7 was more challenging, with geometry and some simple algebra. But he would pass, he was sure, he was one of the cleverest in his class and a diligent student. They sat for another hour or two, easy in each other's company, until Jackson's aunt called from inside the house – time to take Veronica home.

They walked through the warren of houses, Jackson wheeling his uncle's bicycle next to him for the ride home. They reached the main street and found it unusually quiet. It was dark and unlit as usual, with just a white glow from the wooden kiosk where you could charge your phone or buy airtime top-ups. But no one seemed to be around. They walked further on, towards the market. The road in front of them was blocked. Two military pickups parked nose-to-nose across the street; camouflaged soldiers, expressionless, sat on the benches at the back. Putting a hand gently on

Veronica's arm, Jackson steered the bike down a side alley to the left. *Nothing to worry about*, he said; they would take the back route.

"What's happening there?" Veronica whispered, as they turned another corner.

In front of them was the biggest house in Gudele, a two-storey building encircled by a high brick wall topped with razor wire. It was the home of Riek, the ex-vice-president who had been at loggerheads with the government since his sacking in July. Now his residence in the heart of the Nuer district was surrounded by vehicles – a couple of pickups and some white four-by-fours – and around them more soldiers, armed with rifles. Radios crackled on the soldiers' belts but there was a strange, background quiet that chilled the teenagers. Everyone else around seemed to have retreated to their homes, with doors shut up.

"We're going back," Jackson instructed, turning the bike to retrace their steps.

"What? But where?" asked Veronica, frightened now, a feeling that recalled the flash of terror she had experienced when they told her that her father was dead.

"Back to my house. We can't go through here."

"But what about my mother?" Veronica replied urgently. "I have to go home!"

Jackson quickened his pace and Veronica had no option but to jog beside him, back up the main street, turning into the little unmarked lane that led to his home. His jaw was set and he said nothing as he fast-walked home. By the time they reached his aunt's house, Veronica was out of breath. That's when they heard the first gunshots.

CHAPTER 4

Daniel

December 2013

The pickup delivered Daniel and the others just as it was getting dark. The colonel's homestead in Bor was a symbol of the family's relative wealth. Inside its stick-fence perimeter stood half-a-dozen grass thatched huts arranged like satellites around a sturdy, tin-roofed house – its door bolted and padlocked, because the colonel wasn't there. In his absence, the compound was home to Daniel's father's first wife, several aunties, their children, a drunken cousin and a brood of chickens. The menfolk, with the exception of the useless cousin, were away, grazing the cattle.

Daniel had been born in this place, but his visits home had been rare since then. He felt embarrassed that he could barely identify the relatives who had lined up to greet them. Their arrival was unexpected. His father's first wife, pulling a shawl around her shoulders, was coolly polite.

"You are welcome," she said flatly, as the truck that had delivered them pulled away in a roar of loose grit. Daniel's young stepmother set her little boy down on the ground and bobbed an awkward curtsey in the direction of her senior counterpart. Daniel, unsure of the etiquette, bowed his head.

They were ushered to the fire and served warm *kisra,* peppered goat and tea in metal beakers. As best he could, Daniel explained the situation in Juba as his father's wives – his first and his most recent – eyed each other awkwardly over the glowing firewood. His relatives asked questions and murmured their concern.

"The colonel was right to send you," his elder stepmother concluded, rising to retire to bed. "You'll be safe here. Tomorrow we'll slaughter a chicken to welcome you properly."

Her prediction was wrong. It took just a few hours for the war to catch up with Daniel. It began with a distant rumble, like thunder, but soon exploded into the whistle and crunch of artillery rounds and bursts of gunfire. Daniel squatted in the doorway of one of the huts, not comfortable in or out. As dawn broke, family members started to emerge, terrified. They were just as unfamiliar to him in daylight, Daniel thought as he tipped the plastic jerrycan for a handful of water and cleaned his face. He remembered his father's words, the maxims every Dinka boy was expected to live by. "Never be a coward," his father had said. "If someone wants to hurt your brother, you will push your brother behind you and say 'do it to me'. That is how we live."

There was no discussion, no plan, but everyone seemed to

know they had to get out. They started to gather at the gate, more than a dozen of them, the biggest family in Bor town, the richest and most respected. They had to leave, they knew it, but the world beyond the fence was hostile now. The only escape was the river, and even that was uncertain territory. The earth trembled, there was a volley of rifle fire, shouting – the soldiers must be in the marketplace. Five minutes and they'll be here, Daniel thought.

"You, next, run!" commanded his cousin, the one with liquor on his breath, who had assumed authority as the eldest man in the group. Daniel kicked off his flip-flops, glanced left and right, scooped up little Akuei and ran, head down, towards the tall reeds on the riverbank.

The ground was gnarly and uneven. He'd made the right decision to go barefoot, the plastic sandals would have tripped him up by now. His half-brother bounced on his shoulder – was that him whimpering? He heard gasping inside his own head and the crack of bullets behind him, around him. A Nuer fighter was after him, he was sure, but Daniel was running away, accelerating now, faster than he knew he could.

"Here!" barked a young cousin, one of the first to reach the thick river grasses, twice as high as them. Daniel put down the little boy whose legs quivered as he tried to stand. They held back the elephant grass to show the others their hiding place. Daniel's young stepmother raced to her son, then came two wives of his uncles, the younger girls, one holding a baby, the boys, more relatives he didn't know and finally his red-eyed elder cousin, breathless from the unfamiliar exertion.

Now through the grasses to the pontoon – the usual track

was far too exposed. The reeds scratched their arms and legs and the spiky shoots at the base speared their bare feet. But they advanced wordlessly, they knew where they were going. Daniel kept in line.

"Always be brave. You stand and face it." His father's words again. Again came gunfire, the crack and boom of heavy weapons. How did they find themselves here? This group of disparate family members – cousins, aunties, second wives and their confused children. They felt the cool Nile water on their feet, rising up through the reeds. They had to make their way left, upstream, to the pontoon. It was further than they thought. Akuei was crying and so was the baby, who had been passed to one of the men to carry. Daniel's forearm was bleeding from a cut below the elbow, his feet were shredded and screaming in pain, but he kept pushing back the stiff grass, clearing the way for the ones behind him.

"It's here!" a cousin blurted out, catching his breath as he swung himself around the last grasses to a wooden deck where the boats were moored. They could see two men already paddling furiously to the west bank. Daniel's family members started to jump into one of the big dug-out canoes. Were they their own? No one was sure. The group was feeling the lack of leadership. "We'll take these two!" the senior cousin declared. They split themselves unevenly between two boats, which pitched and wobbled as they clambered in. The strongest among them, including Daniel, picked up paddles and they eased away from the bank, the rising sun, the fighting and the danger at their backs.

Their destination was the place across the river to where the family would retreat when Bor was at its hottest. The dry season in the town could be unbearable. The air would sting like a blowtorch, the food stocks were low, tempers were short. Daniel's father owned some land on the west bank, near the fishing grounds, where the women and children would stay for a couple of months each year, enjoying the balm of the river breeze through woven bamboo-walled huts. They kept a small stock of maize flour there; they could catch fish. Even sleeping on the floor, they would all be fine until this silly skirmish died down.

They reached the far shore and hurriedly tied up the boats. Daniel clambered up the bank and lay down, his breath racing, his feet stinging. Some of the young children were crying, in shock after such a frenetic, bewildering start to the day. The women collected water from the river, dressed the injuries and tried to soothe the children. Daniel stood up gingerly, hobbling on the edges of his feet. He and his cousin opened up the two bamboo houses and pulled out a couple of low wooden chairs.

Daniel was a stranger to these people, his extended family in South Sudan. He was only two when he went off with his mother's family, and the Bor relatives thought he had been lost for good. When he emerged again, they discovered he was studying at a fancy boarding school in Uganda. Daniel knew he had a reputation in the family for being indulged – a bit unfair, he thought.

"So, soft boy, how are you enjoying your holiday?" his cousin jibed as they collapsed into seats strung with cow hide. "You didn't expect a quiet time in South Sudan, did you?"

CHAPTER 5

Veronica

December 2013

Jackson's aunt let Veronica stay and share her bed, partitioned off from the rest of the tiny house by a cotton curtain. Jackson lay on his woven mat just a few feet away and Veronica could hear his uneven breathing; he was awake too. Except for Aunty, who had inexplicably fallen asleep and was now softly snoring, it seemed as if the whole city was awake.

The first rattle of gunfire, which came from the direction of Riek's house, multiplied like a virus, and by the early hours Veronica couldn't tell where the shooting was coming from – it seemed to be all around them. Streets that were usually quiet during the hours of darkness, except perhaps for the bark of a street dog, were alive with confusion and fear. News, unverified and quickly distorted, spread fast between neighbours in Gudele.

"The Tigers have given guns to the Dinka boys," shouted

one on the phone to his brother who lived near the president's compound. "They are looking for Nuer. Anyone who can't answer in Dinka will be taken."

From the clatter and the urgent whispers, the family next door seemed to be dismantling their house completely, piling the tin kettle, saucepans and utensils into their wheelbarrow. The old lady opposite was sobbing and wailing.

"No! Don't take me!" she cried. "I would rather die in my bed."

Veronica, still in her clothes, sat up and pulled back the curtain. Until this moment, she had had absolute faith in Jackson's superior wisdom in everything from grammar to geometry to choosing the best grain in the market. But once she got close enough, she saw panic in his eyes. His silence was permission enough for her to take charge. Adrenalin made her feel clear-headed and strong. She knew they could not stay here. Her mother had told her about how it was in the past, what she had seen in the war. Veronica knew how it worked. Jackson was sixteen but could be taken for eighteen, twenty even. If they found him they would kill him; if they found her they would beat her and rape her.

She shook Aunty from her sleep while Jackson scrabbled under the bed for his uncle's folder that contained their documents. Aunty was proving hard to rouse; sleep was a coping mechanism that she had perfected as a child growing up in southern Sudan: when the war came, the bullets and flames, she could fall into a deep, real slumber and cut it all out, and she could still do it now, all these years on. Veronica was rough, she shook the woman's shoulders, shouting at her in Nuer. "Stand up, Aunty! We need to go! It's not safe!" The woman rose unsteadily to her feet, patted her hair down as she always did when she awoke, and stepped into her plastic sandals. Jackson unbolted the door and they were about to run when Aunty remembered her box. The locked metal box where she kept her chapati takings – all the money she had. It was back in the bedroom, on the far side, where she slept. Jackson went back and retrieved it. "Right," said Veronica firmly. "We stick together."

The blackness was disorienting. Until tonight, Veronica had never been out after dark in Juba. The city was insecure at the best of times. The world's newest capital had the unpredictable atmosphere of a frontier town – its population transient, its communities untrusting – and everyone dirt poor. There were robberies and rapes; except for the sex workers, the night-time city was a no-go zone for women. Even when there was peace, it was heavily militarised and the soldiers could be ill-disciplined, especially when they had been drinking. And the United Nations peacekeepers on the base, they had their own reputation . . . but Veronica knew there was nowhere else to go. They had to get themselves to the UN base near the airport, that was the only safe place for them now.

Veronica had been to the compound at Tomping before. Her brothers played football there and she had been to watch a tournament last year. It was known as UNMISS – a mini-city of shipping containers converted to offices, storerooms, dormitories and toilet blocks. The quickest way was along the main road, but they could hear shots coming from there; it felt like they were encircled by fighting. They would have to weave through the houses, through the slum alleys and across patches of waste ground, trying not to lose direction. Others were doing the same, small groups sprinting across any open spaces, stumbling on the uneven ground, their heads bowed against the gunfire puncturing the air around them. Fires were burning everywhere, the air was choked and grainy. Turning a corner, they saw a group of soldiers ahead, jumping down from a vehicle. Veronica grabbed the others and pulled them back behind a brick hut. She leaned for a moment against its cool wall, closed her eyes and inhaled the acrid smell of explosives. They had to keep moving. They started up the next alleyway – two teenagers and a middle-aged woman moving stealthily, purposefully, through the dangerous city.

Half an hour later and they approached the junction where the Gudele road met the newly tarmacked street that ran up to the base. They crept along a narrow alley between the corrugated roofed stalls that lined the main road. They wanted to check the junction, get their bearings, make sure they were in the right place. A battery light from one of the stores shed a greenish glow at the entrance to the alleyway. Something had been dumped there, blocking their way. Jackson was at the front, advancing carefully to make as little sound as possible. He stopped still and spun around, raising his hand to halt the others. Too late. Veronica was on his shoulder. Her eyes, adjusted to the darkness, quickly absorbed the scene at her boyfriend's feet.

Three men – or they could have been boys – their bodies contorted unnaturally in death. They were piled together, limb on limb, naked and mutilated. One face looked up at them, the head at a freakish angle as if it had been turned sharply on its neck. Veronica could see the dotted *gaar* scarring across the forehead that marked him as a Nuer.

For a moment, Veronica was surprised that her body had accepted what it had seen. She had even started to consider how they could manoeuvre around the obstacle when she felt the bile rise in her throat. Her hands on her knees, she retched, vomit splattering her pink skirt, her sandalled feet and the men's bodies. Her breathing quickened and she started to make a noise, a strangled yelping, building up, gaining strength, she needed to scream. She wiped the back of her hand across her lips, gasped in air, raised her neck, opened her mouth. Suddenly she stumbled backwards, her head spinning. A stinging heat burned her left cheek and she tasted a metallic trickle of blood in her mouth.

The slap of Aunty's hand had silenced her. The woman, who had barely spoken since they left the house, glared at Veronica, her chest heaving.

"Follow me," she instructed.

For the rest of the journey, Veronica seemed to be floating above her body, which whimpered and stumbled as Jackson cajoled her on. Fires blazed around them; it felt like they were walking head on into the gunfire that clattered in angry exchanges. They kept to the road, darting into side streets to avoid the marauding soldiers, but blocking the way just thirty metres from the UN base was a pickup truck, uniformed soldiers on the flatbed. They had to pass them. Aunty put down her belongings and raised her hands first, and Jackson and Veronica followed her lead. The soldiers were amused.

"So, who are you? Where are you heading at this time of night?" one of them called out in Dinka.

Jackson, who had grown up with Dinka playmates, answered in their language, clear and unaccented.

"We are just civilians. My sister is sick so we are taking her to the medical centre," he said softly.

The soldiers didn't buy it, but seemed sated from the night's killing. One climbed down, his AK-47 on a strap on his shoulder, camouflage jacket open, face sweaty, eyes shining. He came so close that Veronica could see his pulse pumping in his neck. He stared, seemingly admiring her. Veronica felt the sting of where Aunty had struck her and swallowed the acidy vomit in her throat. She stared back. She locked her knees to keep herself upright; she thought she might faint. The soldier smiled, turned to Jackson, paused and spat in the boy's face. Silence. Veronica dipped her head, hoping that Jackson wouldn't do anything stupid. He stayed immobile, holding the soldier's gaze. Aunty stood like a statue. The soldier laughed, spun round on his army boots and walked back to the truck. Cautiously, the three civilians walked on to the blue UN gates.

CHAPTER 6

Daniel

December 2013

Daniel stood on the riverbank and jabbed the button on his phone again. He was struggling to get through to his father. The first time it had rung out with no reply; how could he not pick up? He knew his father had a habit of blacklisting certain numbers so as not to be disturbed at important moments, but he thought that was only for his wives. He wouldn't do that to his son, surely? He would know about the fighting in Bor by now, there was no question about that. It would be major news – Peter Gadet, the big commander, run out of town. Would his father think they'd done the right thing, going across the river? They'd had no choice – if they'd stayed in town they would already be dead. The richest Dinka family in Bor: the Nuer fighters would be happy to make an example of them.

The lone bar of signal kept dipping in and out and he

couldn't get a connection at all. Daniel walked further down the riverbank. The dry season retreat was in an idyllic spot, on a crook in the Nile where the river meandered through a coconut grove and the water glided past so smoothly the tall, gently swaying trees were reflected perfectly. But Daniel's eyes were fixed on his phone. He held it out over the water, up above his head – anything to try and get a better reception.

A boom concussed through his body. His heart pounded; he felt sick. The explosion must have been miles away but it still made the ground tremble. A tower of smoke rose from the opposite bank; he couldn't see the town from here because of the river bend, but now he heard gunfire in the distance. The Nuer men would storm his father's compound, find it empty, save for the chickens, and they would come and look for them here. His stepmothers, his aunties, their children, it was like they expected him to know what to do, but he didn't; he had never been in a war before and his cousin was no use. They told the worried children they were going to defeat those soldiers and would soon go back home. But all the adults knew that wasn't going to happen. They just didn't know what to do instead.

Daniel looped an arm around the slim husk of a tree trunk and leaned out over the river. The signal was slightly better. He held his other arm out above the water, scrolled through the little grey screen with his thumb and stabbed at his father's number. His hand was sweaty. If he dropped the phone now they would be finished. He brought it back up to his face, trying to read the screen in the dazzling light. He blinked. A little row of repeating dots showed it was connecting. Daniel felt the back of his neck burning. *Please pick up this time, Baba, please.*

In a country where everything was broken, it was hard to explain how sometimes things just worked. Obscure connections of clan, unfathomable networks of patronage and unorthodox channels of communication would somehow align to make the unexpected happen. And so it was that a fisherman upriver near the UN base at Minkamon was persuaded to board his small motorboat that afternoon and chug downstream to rescue Daniel's family, gunfire peppering the water around him as he passed by the smouldering town of Bor.

When he'd finally got through to his father, Daniel had explained the situation in a single breath. They were at the house across the river but they weren't safe. *What should we do, Baba, where should we go?* Daniel's father was typically unfazed. He quickly concocted the plan to pick them up by boat and calmly explained to Daniel what would happen. Daniel had doubts about whether it could work, and seven excruciating hours passed before the little vessel miraculously puttered up to the bank. Not for the first time in his life, Daniel whispered thanks to his father and his seemingly God-like powers. How the colonel had made this happen he would never know, but it didn't matter as they piled into the unsteady craft, the boatman cursing and yelling at them to sit down and to throw out the sleeping mats and baskets of dried fish that Daniel's aunts had insisted upon bringing.

It was dusk when they set off; to reach safety they would have to pass Bor again. As they approached, the fisherman steered into the reeds on the opposite bank, cut the outboard motor and they waited in silence for solid darkness to fall. Whispering thanks again, this time for a black, moonless night, Daniel knelt up in the boat to paddle on the right, the boatman taking the other side. A quick glance to the east and Daniel could see the fires of his ravaged hometown still glowing. The children whimpered with fear and cold. Daniel tried to focus on the gentle splashing of water against his paddle. They were so close to the town now they could hear the jeers and laughter of the conquering soldiers.

They reached Minkamon just before dawn. The family disembarked in silence, the women carrying sleeping children. They had come with nothing. For all of them, this was the start of years of war that would affect them each in different ways. As his cousin had taken pleasure in pointing out, Daniel had always been set apart from the others; compared to them, he led a life of relative privilege. And this time was no exception. While the rest of the family sought sanctuary at the UN base, Daniel's father arranged for his son to be transported back to Juba on an army patrol boat, and from there he sent him back to Arua – and his mother and sister – in Uganda.

CHAPTER 7

Lilian

2014

Lilian was a woman of hope. Everyone felt good around her; she had confidence, a sharp way of thinking and a laugh as clear as a bell. She was youthful and energetic, still in her early twenties, married with a young son. But she also had the tact and perception of a much more experienced woman, which made her perfect for her job at Voice for Change, a grassroots organisation that took her from doorstep to doorstep in the thatched-hut neighbourhoods of Yei. She identified the most vulnerable people among an already impoverished community – the widows, the orphans and the sick. With professional assuredness, she would encourage those most at risk of HIV to get themselves tested, and direct them to where they could access medical assistance. She would train their carers on how to cope with complicated drug therapies, when to administer the pills and explain about the need for good nutrition. She looked out for women and children suffering from domestic violence, quietly taking them aside to listen to their stories and to coax them to seek help.

The troubled caseload helped to cement Lilian's feelings of good fortune about her own life. Her husband Samuel was an engineer. He was kind, gentle and funny. He was the only man she had ever been intimate with; she loved being with him. She knew what it was like for some of the other women, but Samuel would never force himself upon her or hurt her. They had met young, when they were both alone in the world. Their relatives had been scattered in the long independence struggle that had blown apart so many families. Lilian was still at school when her mother had taken off for Uganda. Their other parents were dead, siblings had fallen out of contact, so their wedding was a small affair witnessed by an elderly aunt, some cousins and a few church friends. Lilian wore a wax-print dress in turquoise, orange and yellow, her hair braided with gold beads. There were no photos of that day, but those who were there would always remember how the couple glowed with happiness.

They had a home, a snug, grass-roofed hut in a glade of banana trees. They had chickens and a small vegetable garden. Sometimes they would lie awake all night talking and laughing. In this whole world, Lilian had found the man who fitted her best, right there, in Yei. So when their son was born less than a year after the wedding, Lilian decided to name him Harmony. Samuel thought it was ridiculous, but Lilian knew it was perfect.

In 2014 the war had just begun, but Yei, nestled in the lush forested hills of Western Equatoria, was untouched. Lilian wouldn't have known there was a war at all except there were some things you couldn't get in the market any more. The weather was warm and breezy and they had started to plant out the cassava, sweet potato and beans. Samuel had patched up the roof with bundles of dried grass and cleared the drainage ditch ready for the rains. He wanted to make sure everything was in order. After the weekend he was leaving for the north, near the oilfields. He had a construction contract on a big housing project for oil workers near Bentiu in Unity State. An agent from the company had come to Yei, recruiting for labourers. He was pleased to find a qualified engineer like Samuel, who was to start work on a higher grade. It was good money and Samuel accepted straight away. He wanted to do this for his family. But Lilian had wept when he told her, and so had three-year-old Harmony when he saw his mother cry. Bentiu was about four hundred miles away, and this was South Sudan, a country with no roads. It would take Samuel a week to hitchhike there along the hopeless, pitted dirt tracks which turned to rivers in the rainy season. He'd be gone for at least five months, he told his wife, but it would be worth it: when he returned, he said, they would all get new shoes.

"Samuel, come and look!" Lilian shouted.

Samuel stepped out of the darkness of their home, blinded momentarily by the bright sunshine. When his eyes had adjusted, he saw his wife sitting on a low stool in the shade of the wide-leaved trees. Her face was shining. Little Harmony was jumping around in front of her, a stick in his grubby hand.

"Look what he's done!" Lilian said, pointing to the dirt ground. In big letters, with the 'r' reversed, Harmony had spelt out his name in the red dirt. He was not yet four.

"You have taught him well," Samuel grinned at his wife. She looked up at him. They could not contain their smiles.

"He's not a dull boy," Lilian ventured. She knew her powerful maternal love precluded an objective view, but she thought her son was perfect. Sometimes she couldn't believe he was theirs.

"I think we can say he is very bright," Samuel smiled.

It was his last weekend at home before he set off for the north. The air was fresh; wispy high clouds streaked across a porcelain blue sky. It was just the three of them. On Saturday night they wrung the neck of one of the chickens and roasted it over the fire. There was still plenty left on Sunday, after church. Lilian had packed Samuel's small travelling bag; he had a spare pair of trousers, two shirts, some underwear, a handkerchief, a piece of soap, his wallet and ID card. It hadn't taken long. Neither of them had a phone, but messages would be relayed through the company office in Yei, Samuel had assured her. As soon as the rains were over he would be back. She was to tend the crops and they would harvest them together. She was to keep the door locked. That night, after Harmony had fallen asleep, Lilian buried her wet face in her husband's chest, her shoulders shaking with sobs. He stroked her hair in the darkness.

As soon as he got to Bentiu, Samuel had felt uneasy. He spoke to Lilian on the company phone and joked that he had arrived in bandit country. But she could sense the disquiet in his voice. The Arab *Janjaweed* militia still roamed on horseback to grab what they could and the security forces turned a blind eye. The region had become a flashpoint in the war – there was oil there, so it was inevitable. Oil had enriched the powerful in South Sudan, and to be powerful, you had to have oil. So the fighting between Salva's and Riek's men in Juba had quickly been replicated in the north. Samuel managed to get three phone calls through to Lilian in those first weeks; she was summoned to the office in Yei to receive them. They spoke briefly about the security situation each time, but Samuel was more keen to talk about Harmony and the garden; he didn't have long to speak.

"I think the rain will come next week; you can get the rest of the seeds in now," Samuel said. "The boy can help you!"

"Yes," Lilian replied, her voice cracking. Harmony was standing with her, holding on to her leg. She was stroking his cheek. "We'll do that."

How she wished Samuel hadn't gone. She didn't care about the new shoes. She just wished he was there with her. They had been happy; they had wanted for nothing. In the evenings, when Harmony was asleep, Lilian would listen to the news reports on their FM radio. She had heard about the fighting in Bor and Malakal and now they were talking about Bentiu. She switched off the radio and the cold, white light of the solar lamp. She curled up in bed next to her son. She sang softly into his warm neck until she drifted off too.

*

Strictly speaking, it wasn't the war that killed Samuel, but if it wasn't for the war he probably would have survived. In the lawless, threatening atmosphere that simmered around him, it was every man for himself. Grudges could be settled without consequence. Samuel's body was found by hunters in the bush outside town, far from any roads, just a month after he'd arrived in Bentiu.

When they contacted Lilian, the construction company said he had been missing for three days, which they assumed was how long he had been dead. He still had his ID card in his pocket and a wallet with a photo of Lilian. They sent Samuel's clothes and his few belongings back to her. But they said it was best to bury his body there. There was no formal police investigation – there was a war on. Samuel's company said they thought it was a colleague who had killed him in a dispute over money, a Nuer man who had disappeared on the same day. It was just another killing among so many. Life was disposable in South Sudan. Lilian tortured herself thinking about it, with no one but Harmony to share her grief. She would hug him, rock him and cry into his soft, cropped hair. Harmony didn't cry, but he was quiet for weeks. Lilian made a promise to herself: she would bring up their son to be a good, strong man. That was her mission now, by which she would honour her husband.

CHAPTER 8

Daniel

2015

School was out – forever this time. Eighteen months after his escape from Bor, Daniel had graduated from high school. Like every good South Sudanese boy, Daniel understood that education should be valued above all else, but nevertheless he was overjoyed to be free of the regime at St Augustine's. One of the best private boarding schools in northern Uganda, with good examination results, the formula had changed little since his teachers were at school, or their teachers before them. Overcrowded dormitories, hunger, rudimentary sanitation, teaching by rote, chores, bullying and regular canings were standard. Daniel, a popular outsider with an exotic past, had escaped the worst of it and had graduated with good, if not exceptional, scores – enough, he hoped, to get him into the University of Juba back home. He had discovered a well-worn book about economics in the poorly resourced school library, and had read it twice – he had started to think that was the subject he'd like to study. For now, however, it was time to celebrate his new freedom and enjoy the last few days with his school friends.

Alice was hosting the leavers' party. A few miles from town, her house was upmarket by Arua standards. Her father was working for a Chinese firm in Entebbe, she told Daniel, and sent home money each month. The house had a roof of corrugated iron and a concrete patio decorated with pot plants. Her father was away nearly all year round and her mother usually gave in to Alice's demands. It wouldn't be a big party, Alice had said, and probably no alcohol – no one could afford it anyway. What was important was the music, the dancing and being together, away from school and that stupid rule that insisted that boys and girls keep three feet away from one another at all times.

Alice had put out a white plastic table, as many chairs as she could find and set up another trestle table for the sodas and samosas. Her friend Maureen's brother had brought over the sound system and a diesel generator borrowed from the hair salon in town where she had got new braids that day. Her navy school pinafore had been passed on to her sister, and she was wearing a bright blue pencil skirt and silky sleeveless top that showed off her smooth, elegant arms.

When the boys started arriving in a convoy of *boda-boda* motorbike taxis, Alice's mother said nothing but took the younger siblings to sleep at their aunt's house on the other side of the cassava plot. Alice would be punished when her father found out about this – his phone was probably ringing in Entebbe right now – but that would be another day and the excitement she was feeling was already compensation enough. She put on their high school anthems – "Mama" by Kiss Daniel, "Pray" by Justin Bieber – loud enough to drown out the drone of the generator. At first they all felt a bit awkward together, with this unfamiliar freedom, in this grown-up setting. But soon there were a few jokes at the expense of teachers and other students, and stories about the silly things they had done together. The boys and girls began to mix, the bass was turned up and the dancing started.

Daniel kept smiling. The night air was beautiful, just right, he felt free and so alive. He was on the makeshift dance floor, moving in his usual gawky style, his knees bent, his hips low, but he still towered over the others. Maureen was there, sipping awkwardly on a beer, and so were Aisha and Michelle, dancing hip-to-hip. Daniel inhaled the sour scent of the girls' sweat as they moved around him, but there was nothing going on, they were just having a good time. No one would forget this night.

"Hey, Daniel, get down!" shouted Aisha, who was grinding her hips low to the floor, followed by Michelle and Maureen. Daniel tried to do the same, squatting and twisting his long, skinny legs, and was almost as low as the girls when he lost balance and fell back on the concrete. The girls squealed with laughter.

He propped himself up on his palms, his face bright, sweat shining on his forehead. He was still on the ground when he spotted Joshua stepping out of the low doorway of Alice's house. He watched his friend smooth down his T-shirt and glance around self-consciously. Daniel stared at the door, holding himself in a crab position, the girls dancing happily around him. A minute later and out came Alice, just as he had suspected. Daniel watched them slip back among the dancers. He felt the heady rush of freedom drain from his body.

He got up, walked over to the sound system, and turned down the music.

"Guys, we should go," he said, his voice tight in his throat.

"What?" said Keno, laughing. "Man, we're not going anywhere! Turn the music back up!"

Daniel slumped down in one of the plastic chairs. He suddenly felt sober and anxious. Maybe it was seeing Joshua and Alice together, although he wouldn't admit it, or maybe it was his unarticulated worries about the next chapter of his life. His father hadn't been in touch much recently, and Daniel wasn't really sure whether anyone had given any thought to the next stage of his education, or more importantly, whether there was any money for it. He let a couple more songs play then banged down a half-drunk soda on the speaker.

"Guys, right now, we're going!" he said.

"Relax, man, what's the rush?" replied Keno, who was dancing close to Skovia, a once-shy schoolgirl transformed by black jeans and a shiny gold T-shirt.

"We've got to go; it'll take us an hour to walk. My mother's probably still awake, she'll be waiting for us," said Daniel.

"Seriously, man, cool it," replied Keno, one of the boys from out of town supposed to be staying with Daniel at his mother's small house in Arua. "We're having a good time, you're having a good time, right? We'll go back when it's light!"

Daniel's friend Paul was playing cards at the table with a *boda-boda* boy. Jimmy was with the girls from Dormitory Three. Joshua was dancing with Alice, her thigh braced between his legs.

"Now," Daniel shouted above the music, his voice oddly aggressive. "We're leaving."

Daniel lay on the hospital bed staring up at the bright strip light above his head. He tried not to blink and stared so hard it turned to swimming blotches of brilliant white that stung his eyes and made them water. He didn't blink. It hurt and that's what he wanted. Maybe if he made his eyes hurt enough he would stop feeling the pain from his shattered legs. He had been screaming when he was brought in, the nurse had told him, disapprovingly. He was screaming when they hauled him back on to the trolley and took him for an X-ray. He screamed like a newborn baby, she had said, until they gave him an injection and he came to his senses. Then they had told him about his two broken legs and the fracture in his collarbone. It was his left tibia they were most worried about – a compound fracture, very difficult. He was lucky to be alive, the doctor had said, and lucky he was here in Uganda. What if this had happened in South Sudan? He had laughed. *Were there even hospitals there?*

His mother was sitting on a plastic chair on one side of the bed and his sister on the other. He could smell the charcoal smoke drifting through the metal mosquito grille over the windows. Arua General Hospital did not provide food; the relatives of patients were cooking in the open, preparing soup and maize-meal for the sick. It stank in this ward, like his dormitory at school, stale sweat, urine and disinfectant, so the cooking smoke was almost a comfort. The pain was agonising, he could only manage a couple of words before lying back again, grimacing, his teeth and fists clenched. His mother had no money to pay for medicine, so when the anaesthetic had worn off the pain returned. His father had been called. If Daniel was going to lose his leg, his father would want to be here, his mother had said, as if it was all very normal and straightforward. But Daniel had heard her crying when he closed his eyes and pretended to sleep. She knew as well as he did what this meant. Life for any South Sudanese boy was hard. For a South Sudanese boy with one leg? It was over.

He had finally got the group together – Keno, Paul, Jimmy and lastly Joshua, who was having a momentous night and was the most difficult to extract from the party. They were all puzzled by Daniel's sudden desire to leave and definitely put out by his aggression, but their loyalty to their friend meant they hadn't put up that much resistance – something Daniel would think about later, with the tug of guilt that shrouded all of his memories of that night.

They had set out along the road to Arua – newly surfaced with a dusty track at the side for pedestrians that came and went depending on the terrain. The throb of the party music faded as they walked past clusters of sleeping thatched houses and thick-stumped banana trees silvered by moonlight. The boys were on a high, singing and skipping up the road, every so often breaking into a jog to keep up with Daniel who strode ahead. They were less than a mile from town, at a wide bend that swept around a rocky outcrop. The minibus must have been picking up speed, coming towards them on a straight stretch before it took the corner. The rocks must have created a sound barrier, because no one heard it coming; they all agreed on that afterwards.

"So, Josh, what is *up* with you and Alice?" Keno was teasing. Joshua, delighted, but feigning offence, had started to wrestle his friend to the ground when Daniel turned to tell them to quit. For a split second, the lights from the bus illuminated the scene: the boys, their eyes bright, legs kicking, laughing and breathless as they grappled on the tarmac.

Then bang. Blackness.

The early morning bus from Arua to Kampala had been coming fast, expecting an empty road. It struck Daniel first, knocking him up into the air, and then ploughed into the others before swerving away and coming to a halt in the trees on the other side of the road. Somehow, Jimmy had managed to throw himself in the other direction, against the rocks that hugged the bend. The driver had been wearing his seatbelt, which had served its purpose; the other seven passengers, still sleepy from their early morning start, were hurled forwards, their heads colliding with metal seat backs and luggage. In the front passenger seat, the fare collector, clutching his wad of dirty notes, had come off worst, his neck whipped forward and back; leaving him slumped against the dashboard.

Jimmy stumbled towards the others. He could feel a grating sting on his left cheek where he had hit the rock, his vision was blurred but his limbs were functioning. His friends were scattered on the road. Keno was on his back, his eyes closed. Joshua was on all fours making a small squeaking noise. Paul had blood on his forehead and in his eyes and he was trying to get up. The force of the impact had somehow stripped Daniel's T-shirt off and a leg of his grey jeans was missing. After a few seconds of quiet, Jimmy heard the bang of the minibus door, the driver screaming in Lugbara: "What the fuck! What the fuck were you doing?" He launched himself towards Jimmy, who cowered with his left hand holding the bloodied wound on his face. The driver glowered, his eyes wild, then retreated back to the minibus, hauling open the side door to discover the fate of his passengers.

The sun was not yet up, but a road crash quickly attracts a crowd. With sheer strength of numbers, the bus was quickly righted, set back on the road and transformed to the role of ambulance. The injured passengers remained inside, while the neighbourhood brawn roughly lifted the four boys into the back, overseen by Jimmy, who clambered in after them, weeping as the driver sped angrily towards the hospital.

On the second day Daniel gathered the courage to ask about his friends. Worse than the pain in his leg was the dread he felt about his schoolmates. It was he who had made them walk down that road, in the dark. It was he who had turned the best night of their lives into the worst. He couldn't move or look around but he was sure they weren't in this ward with him. He had shared a dormitory with them for four years, he knew their breathing, their smell, their noises. If they weren't here, what did that mean? They were okay? Or maybe the opposite. He couldn't bear to think about that. The last thing he remembered was that snapshot of Keno and Josh wrestling on the ground, they were so happy, they all were.

Why had he spoiled it? He couldn't remember seeing them on the ride to the hospital, his eyes had been full of blood, and all he could think about was his own pain.

He waited for his mother to go out to use the toilet and wash her face. His sister Tabitha was still there, sitting rigid in her plastic chair.

He cleared his throat, his nails digging into his palms. "Where are the boys?" he whispered.

His sister looked terrified, he thought. She didn't reply.

"Where are they?"

Tabitha burst into tears. She buried her face in her hands and Daniel watched her shoulders shake as she tried to get herself back under control. She knew all those boys, they were two years above her at school; she had watched them grow from football-mad adolescents into the young men they now were.

"They are here," she sobbed. "They are alive."

Daniel let his head sink back on the bare mattress, closed his eyes and let the pain wash back through his body. He held out his hand for his sister to hold, which she did, as she wept with relief and fear. Keno was the worst of them, she said, with a broken leg and arm which had been already splinted and should heal. Joshua and Paul had been luckier, but were badly bruised and cut and would remain in hospital for a few more days. Jimmy was there with them, but none of them had been allowed to visit Daniel, that had been the doctor's instructions.

They were still holding hands when their mother came back to the bedside, looking more stricken than ever, Daniel thought, and in the next moment he understood why.

Tabitha jumped up from her chair; behind their mother was their father, tall and imposing, even in his civilian shirt and trousers. The colonel quickly greeted his daughter by pressing his cheek to hers and sat down in her chair.

Daniel stood to attention as much as he could. He turned his body towards his father, straightened his neck on the mattress and summoned all his strength to conceal the pain that was screaming from his leg. His father glanced up and down at his son's broken body, half covered by a sheet, a catheter line running from under it to a bag under the bed. His mother and sister stood on each side of his father, and Daniel wondered if they had ever been together like this before, just the four of them, alone.

"I've brought a car, Daniel," his father said, without any enquiry about what had happened or how his son was feeling. "I'm taking you back to Sudan. They have already dismissed you here. I have spoken to the doctor. They are not willing to save your leg." His mother looked alarmed, but kept her eyes fixed straight ahead. Daniel knew she would never question his father, and neither could he, but the thought of being moved in this condition filled him with terror.

His father was already striding across the ward to get the attention of a nurse. His mother and sister stood at his bedside; he could see his sister was trembling. They would not be coming with him; past experience had taught them that. His father's old-fashioned English boomed across the ward. He wanted Daniel's notes, his X-rays, some painkillers for the journey and the hospital bill. He would settle it now. The nurse darted in and out of the ward and was almost panting when she scampered back with a manila envelope containing Daniel's X-rays and a blister strip of tablets. Deferentially, she handed them over and invited the colonel to follow her to the cashier's office.

Once his father had left, Daniel's mother grabbed her son's hand and lowered her face to his. "Remember your prayers," she whispered. "Make me proud." Daniel felt his mother's tear fall on his cheek.

CHAPTER 9

Veronica

2013–2014

When Veronica, Jackson and Aunty finally reached safety inside the UN base in Juba they had all felt a moment of euphoria. At seven thirty in the morning, blue-helmeted UN peacekeepers had opened the gates, offering sanctuary to the terrified throng outside. The foreign soldiers had patted them down for weapons, questioning Jackson in detail on his movements since the fighting had broken out. He had answered calmly and respectfully in English; he was good like that.

It wasn't only Nuer like them who had sought refuge – some Dinka were inside too, mostly women and children in small groups, squatting next to the shipping containers that were the peacekeepers' offices and homes. They could still hear the snap of gunshots outside, and the crump of shell-fire further away. They found a spot where they could squat down and wait. Veronica started jabbering about what she had seen and how she had felt at certain points on their journey, exhilarated, as if she had just stepped off a rollercoaster.

"Did you see those men? The dead ones? Did you see them? Did you see their eyes?" she said in horrified wonder.

"Yeah. All Nuer, poor bastards," said Jackson, rubbing the sweat off his forehead with his T-shirt sleeve.

"God rest them," murmured Aunty.

"I can't believe we got here. Feel my hand! I'm still shaking," said Veronica excitedly, suddenly sounding like the child she was. "I thought that soldier was going to cut our throats, honestly I did. Did you see that look in his eyes? He—"

"Shut up," commanded Aunty, hugging her nightdress around her knees, rocking gently back and forth.

Jackson reached for his girlfriend's hand. Veronica clasped on to him tightly, closed her eyes and breathed in and out, trying to calm herself. When she opened them again she looked around and saw more people than she had ever seen in one place before. No one knew what to do, but everyone started forming lines anyway – in front of the main UNMISS office, the canteen and the water taps. By now they all had a desperate thirst, but nothing had been provided. Babies were howling; frightened children whimpered and clung to their mothers' legs. Veronica noticed that the Dinka and the Nuer had instinctively separated themselves, forming their own queues, not speaking, trying not to look at each other. Then she felt a jolt. What was she doing? Why had she not thought about her family? Her mother, her sister, Santino and Simon? She set off up the line.

"Veronica!" Jackson shouted after her. "What are you doing? You can't push in!"

She marched to the top, scanning every face, recognising none. She walked back again, searching faces, ignoring Jackson who tried to pull her back into the queue when she passed him. She went right to the back, and started pacing up other lines, seeing no one she recognised at all. Then she saw one face that looked familiar, a woman from church.

"Aunty," she began respectfully. "I am Veronica, from St Joseph's. I am looking for my mother, she is Elizabeth, I think you know her? And my younger brothers. And my little sister?"

The woman, whom Veronica had only seen in her smart Sunday suit before, was looking wild: shoeless, braless, her hair untamed; and missing a front tooth.

"No, no, I've come alone," she replied flatly, not meeting Veronica's eyes.

"Well . . . if you see them, my mummy and the others, please tell them I am here," Veronica said. "I am with Jackson . . . and his aunt, you know her? She has the chapati stall?"

The woman stared straight ahead. Veronica looked down and saw her own hands trembling. She walked on up the line, and the next; she spent hours wandering the compound until she lost her bearings completely. She had not drunk any water and eventually had to stop to join a queue at a standpipe. A few people had got hold of cups or containers; she would have to cup her hands and drink what she could when she reached the tap, she thought. The sun was rising fast and by mid-morning it was already burning hot. People around her were jostling. She squatted down and tried to make some shade for herself, putting her arms over her head.

"Veronica."

She looked up. Santino, in his white football shirt. Her brother crouched down next to her and started to cry. She hadn't seen him cry since their father died. He was a brave boy. He burrowed into her shoulder, shaking as he tried to hide his face with his hands. She put her arm around him. She never did that. She let him sob and the others in the queue shuffled around the two siblings, huddled together on the ground.

"Mummy and the others are by the football pitch," her brother whispered at last.

Juba's night of terror marked the start of the civil war. Locals preferred to call it *the crisis* – as if a more modulated definition would soften its impact. Although tempered by pauses and peace deals, it was indeed a war – unconventional, unpredictable and complex – with devastating consequences. After the first bout of blood-letting, Juba was quiet but uneasy. Tens of thousands of mostly Nuer civilians remained under the protection of peacekeepers in the UN base, too fearful to leave. The better-off had left for Khartoum, Nairobi and Addis Ababa, while others headed over the border to seek refuge in Uganda. Businesses closed down, banks and shops shut their doors. Prices rocketed and everyone was poor: less than three years after the hope and expectation of independence, the new country was tearing itself apart.

While most Nuer civilians stayed under UN protection at the base, Veronica's mother decided they should go home. She was a true SPLA believer and she couldn't believe this division would last. After a week they walked back to their house in Gudele in the clothes they had been wearing on the night of the fighting: Veronica in her T-shirt and long fuchsia-coloured skirt, her mother and sister in their cotton nightdresses and the boys in their football shirts and shorts. The streets looked different. The air smelt of burned plastic. The stores and shacks that lined the main Gudele Road were smashed up and looted, just heaps of broken brick and mangled corrugated iron. All the hawkers were gone, there were bullet casings, discarded shoes, broken plastic chairs, pools of dried blood and the charred ruins of torched houses. Every thirty metres was a sandbagged position, with two or three soldiers stationed next to a mounted machine gun. Veronica noticed that her mother kept her head down as they passed each one. Usually she would greet her comrades, but not today. All these soldiers were Dinka; where had the Nuer men gone? They walked in silence, Veronica holding her little sister's hand, the boys trailing behind, cautious and arm-in-arm. When they approached their neighbourhood it was hard to work out where their house should be as the usual markers were gone. The phone-charging kiosk on the corner was a blackened heap; so was the Eritrean store, and the butcher's. But then they saw it, their house with the blue iron door, still standing at least— a brief moment of relief that turned to dread as they came closer.

Things were worse than they had feared. Veronica's mother had thought to padlock the door when they had fled the house, but one kick had seen to that. Her mother stepped through the low timber frame, and quickly re-emerged, hand over her mouth, her eyes watering. She ushered the children away with her hand but Veronica dipped her head through the doorway too, and was immediately hit by a frenzy of flies and the stench of faeces. The looters, who had stolen all of their possessions – a cooking pot, soap, mattresses – had left their mark. Veronica backed out of the house, ran around the side and retched. Of course they would clean it up and beg and borrow to replace the items they had lost. They had no choice.

Veronica hated being at home after that. She made excuses and spent as much time as she could with Jackson. The schools did not reopen after the Christmas break, which distressed Jackson who was desperate to pass his primary grades and graduate to the senior years. He tried to spend his days studying, but Veronica claimed her mind was fuzzy and she couldn't concentrate. She thought it was all the shock and upset she'd been through that made her feel sick each morning, light-headed and disoriented. Food prices had soared and there was hardly anything to eat. So when her periods stopped, she decided not to mention it to anyone, not to make a fuss. She'd heard of that happening to other girls when they were hungry.

CHAPTER 10

Daniel

2015

For the first ten minutes, the old man didn't touch him at all. He stood at the end of the cow-skin stretcher on which Daniel lay in constant agony. He waved away the envelope containing the X-rays proffered by Daniel's father and sized up his new patient by eye. He paced slowly around and stared intently at Daniel from the head end, silent and absorbed. Then he ordered his assistant to remove the hopeless dressings on Daniel's legs and watched the young man squirm and grimace and stifle his cries. The old man frowned, a single, deep furrow between cloudy, lashless eyes. He knelt down, placed one hand on each of Daniel's legs and dipped his head as if in prayer.

Daniel's heart pounded, his body still in crisis. He was praying too, desperate to pass out again. Several minutes went by, then the old man stood up in one swift, nimble movement and spat generously on each of Daniel's broken legs, watching with expert curiosity as the trail of saliva slid down towards the stretcher.

Daniel's father and the healer's assistant waited for the diagnosis in expectant silence.

The old man sighed. "You are very stubborn," he said to Daniel at last. "It seems that you don't like to listen to your father or your mother."

He ordered his assistant to splint Daniel's legs and apply a little neem oil. The treatment to save his legs had begun.

Daniel could only remember flashes of the journey from the hospital in Arua to the healer's village in South Sudan. Lying across three seats in the back of the van driven by his father, he dipped in and out of consciousness, sometimes willing himself to live, sometimes to die. The intensity of the pain pushed his mind to places he had never been – from febrile heavenly visions to hellish scenarios that would haunt him even after the pain had gone. It took three days. The last stretch was the worst, when the gravel road ran out and the colonel had to chart a course along a stony stream bed. The minivan, with a strawberry-shaped air freshener suspended from the rear-view mirror and hand-stitched curtains at the windows, was designed for leisure trips, not off-road terrain. It made excruciatingly slow progress as it banked high along the sandy ridges of the narrow riverbed and then crashed back to the centre, axles scraping over the rocky deposits and wheels spinning over the loose stones. In the back, crudely tied to the seats to stop him falling, Daniel suffered a cruel, extended torture.

The colonel had taken his son out of a hospital ward in Uganda and had driven him hundreds of miles away to a village crouched in the wild scrublands of Jonglei State to see an old man. When Daniel's father arrived at Arua General, the doctors had been dismissive. The left leg could not be saved, they had told him, they would amputate, below the knee. The doctors had expected the family to be grateful. The colonel had other plans. It was a matter of pride. He would not see his son mutilated, especially there, in a foreign land. Raised and trained on the battlefields of the Sudanese bush, the colonel had his own way of thinking. He needed to take Daniel home, and would take him directly to the old *mzee* – the man who had removed shrapnel from the colonel's side and saved his life years before Daniel was born.

Jerking and jolting along the gravel roads, mud tracks and stony trenches, the colonel had time to tell Daniel all about the healer. The old *mzee* was a man whose curative powers had become legendary among the guerrilla fighters of the independence struggle, a man whose fabled reputation had warranted the colonel's decision to abandon conventional medicine and strike out to a speck on the map. Daniel was aware that his father was shouting from the driver's seat, telling him about this man whose village was their destination. Daniel vaguely wondered why. Perhaps his father was trying to stop him losing consciousness, perhaps his father needed to justify to himself why he had embarked on this mercy mission. Whatever the reason, Daniel tried to listen – but the words seemed to wash over him.

The old *mzee* was born shortly after the Second World War, Daniel's father said, when southern Sudan was still under Anglo-Egyptian rule. He had been a quiet, knowing boy whose unearthly sensitivity became apparent at an early age. When he was just four his mother watched him cup the tiny, perfect foot of his baby brother in his hand and look up stricken, tears welling in his eyes, as if he had been given a terrible shock. For hours he massaged the baby's smooth soles, gently and carefully, so the infant fell into an easy slumber. But the little boy was still anxious, watching over the baby all that day and the next, stroking him, massaging him and ignoring his mother's encouragement to play outside. On the third day, the woman felt the heat on her baby's forehead, a sign of the fever his brother knew had been coming. The boy looked at his mother imploringly, he wanted to continue his treatment, he knew he could save his brother with his healing hands if she would give him the chance. But his mother did not hand over the care of her baby to his four-year-old brother, of course not. Like all sick children in the village the baby was taken to the old mama, a practitioner of traditional medicine who prescribed herbs and blessings to the sick. But she did not have the boy's powers, he already knew that. For days he paced around the old woman's hut where his mother and the baby had been admitted under the shaman's care. His father came in and out, but the boy was instructed to remain outside. He ignored the calls of his young friends who were wrestling in the dirt and kicking around a football. He kept a vigil through the nights, sleeping on the ground near the doorway, listening for sounds from his baby brother. A week after the boy had felt the first warning emanate from the baby's foot, he was sitting on a tree log in his shorts that were the colour of dust, his strings of red, yellow and black beads hanging around his neck. He stared at the old woman's house. He could just make out the drone of her incantations, calling on departed ancestors for help. When the evening came and fires were lit across the village, he heard his mother's strangled wail. A little later, in the golden twilight, the old lady brought out the lifeless bundle, wrapped in a white shroud.

It would take the family a year to pay off the debt to the woman, in the form of a single, live, healthy goat. The boy knew he could have saved his brother. As he grew older, his powers were slowly acknowledged in the village and mothers would bring their sick children to him, not to the old mama. He could lure guinea worms from blistered hands and feet like a snake charmer, ease malarial fevers, heal jaundice, restore sight and set broken bones. He knew when his sisters were about to menstruate and when women in the village had fallen pregnant. Other women, desperate to conceive, had heard of his powers and would walk for miles to visit him so he could lay his healing hands on their barren wombs. There were no potions, spells or dances. The boy had a gift.

When the first civil war broke out in southern Sudan the boy was a still a teenager. His practice quickly moved on from tending to bodies ravaged by sickness to those blown apart by bullets and grenades. The first soldier brought to him had never stood a chance, he had lost his leg right up to the groin, but his heart kept beating for two more days. That was a lesson for the healer. He felt helpless, impotent in those early days, presented with these freakish man-made injuries – pulsating guts, mangled limbs and blown-off faces, each a gory token of war. He honed his skills, taught himself surgery and experimented with medicinal oils. He was creative, looking to nature for solutions if he could not find the potency he needed within himself. By the early 1960s, when the war had spread from Equatoria to Upper Nile and Bahr-el-Ghazal, the healer ran his own one-man field hospital. He had no drugs, anaesthetics or surgical equipment but commanded the absolute faith of his patients, some of whom had been carried for days from the frontline for a chance of survival.

Through the pain, Daniel understood he had been brought back to South Sudan to be healed. He had never questioned his father and would not have done so now even if he'd had the strength. His father was still talking when the minivan bumped into the village, its headlights illuminating the velvety darkness with a weak, yellow beam. They had arrived unannounced, but a welcoming guard of sleepy villagers soon gathered. It was too late for the *mzee* to be disturbed, they said, but a sleeping mat was found for them in one of the village huts. By the light of a kerosene lamp, his father and a silent young man with an eager, gap-toothed grin carried Daniel through the narrow doorway of a hut and set him down. That night, lying next to his murmuring father in the pitch dark, Daniel felt thirsty, weak and dreamy. He inhaled the smell of woodsmoke and the damp earth beneath them that told him he was back in his homeland.

In the morning, when the old man had completed his first examination, Daniel noted with detached interest that his pain seemed to override all other feelings. He had barely given any thought to the correct way a Dinka should behave in such circumstances; he had not worried about being brave, about inhabiting the correct persona, he simply wanted the pain to end in the quickest way possible. When his new doctor had left his bedside, Daniel turned his head and retched. His stomach clenched up in effort but produced nothing.

His father squatted down and put his hand on Daniel's cheek, wet with tears.

"Don't worry, son," he said, with a tenderness that Daniel found surprising. "This is the place where you will walk again."

When he was a little boy and had imagined his father, Daniel had thought of all the kind words his father would say to him and the playful times they would spend together. But by the time they found each other again, Daniel was too old for childish things, his father had said. He had focused instead on instructing Daniel about everything he had missed. The colonel was dependable and conscientious but never displayed the affection that Daniel craved. When the gestures of love finally came, however, Daniel didn't have the strength to respond. He looked blankly at his father and closed his eyes.

CHAPTER 11

Veronica

August 2014

The midwife pinched Veronica's nipple between the fingers of her left hand and gave the baby's head a gentle push towards it. Veronica looked down to see the frantic effort in her baby's cheeks. She had become a mother at the age of fourteen, going on fifteen. Not that there was time to reflect on this milestone moment. The day had brought intense pain, fear and shame. Her body was her only property, the only thing that truly belonged to her. Now it felt as if this had been taken too.

Veronica had been nearly six months along before she admitted she was pregnant. It was a mixture of denial and ignorance that had stopped her from questioning why she felt nauseous, dizzy and detached. It wasn't until Jackson had mentioned her thickening waistline did she accept the truth. She was long-limbed, tall and lean – eventually there was no way to disguise the perfect but incongruous round belly that grew a little bigger each day. Her mother had been furious. When her school reopened she was made to sit apart from the other pupils and, worst of all, she was banned from seeing Jackson. She was given a cursory ante-natal check at the local clinic and was told nothing at all about what to expect. When her waters broke one Sunday while she was running an errand for her mother after church, she felt the warm, wet rush between her thighs, assumed it was blood, and wondered if the baby had followed too. She stopped and knelt down carefully on the roadside and tried not to draw attention to herself. She checked the damage to her skirt; it was wet but not bloodied, there was no baby but she could see a damp trail in the red dirt behind her. Had she lost control and urinated right there on the street? Her pregnancy had thrown up nothing but awful surprises so far. She stood up carefully and hurried home.

Veronica's mother silently inspected her after listening to a tearful description of what had happened. Soon after, the pain came: first a deep and distant warning and then a regular, angry siren. It was time to go to the clinic. There was nothing to pack. Her mother took Veronica's arm and the pair walked in silence, stopping at intervals for Veronica to double over, gripping her mother's hand, as pain consumed her.

When she arrived they pulled off the skirt that Veronica had been wearing with the waistband pushed below the bump. Then they removed her underwear. She was on the thin plastic mattress of the bed, no sheet, no cover. The midwife pulled a curtain around them, pushed Veronica's knees apart and examined her with a latex-gloved finger. Veronica gasped, not in pain but shame. The ward was busy: she could hear women shrieking in labour, nurses giving instructions, visitors chattering. Veronica thought about the soldiers who patrolled town, the ones she feared and resented. She wished one would walk in now! She would beg him to come over and shoot her. The pain seared inside her, red hot, the skin on her belly taut and prickly. As the spasm eased off, the shame took hold again – an escalating cycle of fear and agony. The next contraction, and Veronica turned involuntarily onto her front, kneeling on the bed, supporting herself on her arms, the plastic sheet repelling her sweat and tears.

It continued for hours. Her mother stayed with her, standing next to the bed, silent and stony-faced. When it was already dark, a midwife came back, a different one, an older woman, in a blue nurse's uniform with a wide white collar. She strapped a blood pressure cuff around Veronica's arm, pumped the bellow and watched the dial as the air slowly deflated.

"What is your name, child?" It was the first time Veronica had been asked this since she had been admitted.

"Veronica Joseph," Veronica whispered with effort as the pain gripped her again.

The midwife was putting on the plastic gloves. Veronica felt terror.

"I need to examine you, to see how you are progressing."

Veronica couldn't reply. This midwife was gentler, more solicitous. She felt between Veronica's legs with a frown of concentration and then looked up with a reassuring smile.

"You are nearly there, child," she said, disposing of the gloves into a metal bucket. "We'll take you to the delivery room."

The midwife stepped out of their curtained cubicle and returned with a folded, cotton sheet. Veronica, at the peak of a contraction, grabbed at it and desperately fumbled to unfold it over her. Wordlessly, her mother came to her assistance and at last Veronica's naked body was covered.

The delivery room was hot and brightly lit. There was a small window with mosquito wire built into the bricks above head-height. Veronica could hear the evening rain beating down outside; it was a comfort. She was on the blue polythene delivery bed. How she hoped this was nearly over. Waves of pain were convulsing her young body every minute or so. She was drifting in and out of awareness. The midwife was back again, the one who had been kind. She eased Veronica's legs apart.

"It's time, child," the woman said. She was attentive but not panicked.

"The next time the pain comes I am going to ask you to push. You take in a deep breath, then you push, then you breathe, then you push. You push hard. You need to be strong."

She placed one hand on top of Veronica's fingers and the other on the taut bump. Her mother looked on, and Veronica noticed her mother's eyes were darting now, from the wall to the floor to her daughter and then the midwife. There was silence for a few seconds and the pain rose again.

"Now breathe and push!" the midwife instructed. Veronica gulped in air and felt the midwife's hand pressing down on her belly. She pushed, as hard as she could, letting out a wild grunt as she felt the veins pop in her face.

"And again!" the midwife shouted. Veronica pushed again, with all her might. The pain receded and Veronica was thrown back into reality, panting from the effort.

"Next time harder, child," the midwife said, squeezing her hand with encouragement.

"No. Not like this," Veronica replied. She heard her words in the air. Even now, in this state, she felt uncomfortable answering back to authority. "I must turn," she explained softly.

The midwife understood. She helped Veronica turn on to her knees on the bed.

"Take her arm!" she ordered Veronica's mother. Her mother complied and with the midwife supporting her on the other side, Veronica manoeuvred herself to a squat just in time for the next contraction.

"Now push! It is coming!"

Veronica pushed again, straining, groaning, her face contorted in pain. She felt stronger now, and pushed again at the midwife's encouragement. The midwife had pulled herself onto the delivery bed, kneeling behind her, in full concentration. To Veronica's horror she took a steel scalpel from the trolley next to her.

"I just need to make a small cut. Stay still child."

Veronica felt nothing, but saw the fresh blood drip onto the blue plastic. There was no time for questions. The pain soared again and Veronica let out a roar as her adolescent body strained with sinewy power. Then a sudden release as she saw the baby, pallid in its slimy coating, slide into the midwife's hands.

Veronica bore the humiliation of the afterbirth – which she had no idea was coming – and of being stitched up in front of her silent mother with resolve. The midwife had cut the cord, then summoned another nurse who came in to weigh the baby, clean its face and swaddle it in a white cloth while the midwife carefully repaired Veronica and dabbed the wound with iodine. The baby was presented to Veronica for feeding. It was a girl. Veronica had not asked.

The midwife tilted her head to see if the baby had latched on properly to her mother's breast.

"What will you call her?" she asked Veronica.

The new mother had not given it a moment's thought.

"I don't know," she replied quietly, observing her new daughter with mild curiosity.

So much had happened, so quickly. Veronica couldn't believe she had been at church that morning and now, at the end of this most bewildering of days, she was here, in hospital, a new life in her arms. Suddenly she looked up. The name had come to her.

"Sunday," she said, firmly. "Her name is Sunday."

CHAPTER 12

Lilian

2016

It was two years since Samuel's death. Lilian believed her husband was looking down on her and she hoped that he would be pleased with what he saw. She had picked herself up and carried on, with Harmony at the centre of her world. She had repaired the house herself and tended their smallholding, even planting out sweet potatoes last season which had done well. Thanks to her efforts, Harmony could read fluently even before his first day of school. After a short break for grieving, Lilian had gone back to work at Voice for Change, much to the relief of the women who had come to depend on her. Despite her sudden, brutal bereavement, Lilian still thought of their problems as being greater than hers. That was her nature.

After work, Lilian played with Harmony in the shady spot outside their little house. He liked the toy truck his father had made him and the metal frame of an old bicycle wheel he pushed with a stick. Lilian could not afford books, but had kept every one of her old school exercise books, dozens of them, piled on the floor with their faded pink, blue and green covers. She would pick one out, slap off the dust and they would go through it together, reading stories that Lilian herself had written as a child or solving maths problems for children twice Harmony's age. He was eager to learn and never complained about his mother's tutoring; he basked in her attention. But his favourite thing was to talk about his father. He would ask so many questions, about his father's voice, his walk, what he liked to eat. What did his laugh sound like? Did he have a favourite goat? He especially loved it when Lilian described how his father would play with him when he was a baby.

"He would throw you in the air, this high!" she said, stretching her arm above her head. "Then he would catch you. His hands were so big. I would scold him when he did that but you were always giggling. You loved it so much."

Sitting on the ground, hugging his knees, Harmony would revel in his mother's memories of his father. How they had the same walk, the same gestures, the same eyes with charcoal rims. If ever she seemed to be coming to the end of a story, he would quickly ask another question.

"How tall was my Baba? Could he ride a motorbike? Did he like snakes?"

The civil war brought hunger and displacement to other parts of South Sudan, but the lush hills and valleys around Lilian's hometown of Yei were at first spared the fighting. It was here that an uprising in 1955 had pitched the South into its first conflict with the government of Khartoum. Two, even three generations had known little else but war until a peace agreement was signed in 2005. In the subsequent decade of calm, the fertile land had bloomed and the children had gone to school without fear.

Yei was by South Sudanese measures a cosmopolitan place. Close to the borders of Uganda and Congo, its residents were mostly from the country's smaller ethnic groups: Lilian's Kakwa tribe, the Kuku, Madi and more. Many of those displaced in South Sudan's earlier conflicts had decided to make their home in the town, attracted by its mild weather, trading potential and verdant hinterland. Hotels and guest houses sprung up to accommodate travelling traders from as far afield as Kinshasa and Khartoum. While it was a stretch of the imagination to compare Yei's dusty main drag to London's Oxford Street, the town had acquired the nickname of "Small London" in recognition of its pleasant climate and relative metropolitan buzz.

The battles in the capital Juba, only about a hundred miles away, hadn't affected Lilian or her neighbours much. Some people had returned home from the capital, complaining it was unsafe and too expensive. The fighting between South Sudan's two main ethnic groups, the Nuer and Dinka, had spilled over to the country's north and east, but Yei was untouched. Ironically, it was a truce signed in 2015 between Salva and Riek that laid the ground for the unravelling of peace in the town. Under the deal, both sides were allowed to establish bases for their troops across all parts of South Sudan, allowing for the deployment of rival forces across

Equatoria. The mostly Dinka soldiers of the government's SPLA controlled the towns like Yei, while Riek's militias held sway in the countryside.

Both sides intimidated and harassed the locals. They extorted food and money and tried to recruit young men to their forces. One day Lilian saw a teenager, who lived near her, staggering home, holding his left arm, his face bruised and swollen. He was a *boda-boda* driver who took people around the sandy lanes of Yei on his grandfather's Chinese-made motorbike. She didn't see him or the bike again after that.

The stage was set for an explosion of violence. It came when the peace deal fell apart in July 2016 and fighting broke out again in Juba. Riek fled the capital through Western Equatoria's forested hills, stoking an insurgency as he marched to Congo with his men. In Yei, the atmosphere quickly turned toxic. Government soldiers went on the counter-offensive, massacring civilians. Families tried to leave by road to Uganda but were turned back by the SPLA: *Why are you leaving? Are you with the rebels?* Those who managed to get away risked ambush, by both sides, and horror stories of cut-throat executions and roadside rapes soon filtered back to town. There were gun battles on the streets, the schools closed, the soldiers ransacked the shops. Old grudges were revived. If a neighbour was in debt to another, or someone had once stolen the other's goat, they would soon be accused of being rebel loyalists, traitors. There were screams in the night as whole families were rounded up, while those left behind lived in terror of what might be next.

Lilian didn't know the family opposite her very well, a couple with three young children, but they had never caused her any trouble. They were not Kakwa like her, they were from somewhere out east, but they seemed pleasant enough. Lilian was woken by the shouts, then the bang of a door being kicked in. She listened, her body tensed, Harmony still sleeping next to her. She heard the muffled screams, then gunshots. She waited for quiet. She stood up, shaking, turned on the torch and looked around the house. What should they take? Some clothes, her schoolbooks, her school certificate, a photo of Samuel, a mirror, shoes. She packed the bag. Then she took the saucepan, the five-litre jerrycan, two kilos of rice. She sat on the edge of the bed. She waited. As a hint of light crept around the door, she woke her warm son from a mist of sleep, kissed his forehead and quickly dressed him. She picked up the saucepan in one hand, the rice bag and jerrycan in the other. She looked at the big bag on the floor, full of her most precious belongings. She left it there.

They walked all day. They kept off the main road, finding others along the way, all with the same intention, moving south, heading to Uganda. Some brought the things they could not bear to leave: a solar panel, a rolled mattress, a bicycle. They were walking through rebel territory; Lilian had seen a couple of their men, dozing by a burnt-out campfire, but there had been no trouble. Harmony had never walked this far, nor had he gone a day without food like this, but he was trying to be brave. By mid-afternoon they had almost reached Ombachi, a small settlement with a school and a church, where they would stop for the night. There were cars there that could take them to the border. Harmony was starting to stagger, Lilian saw, weaving along the path like a drunkard, struggling to keep up. But they had to get there. *Come on my darling, hold my hand. Let's keep going. Not far now. We can rest soon.*

CHAPTER 13

Daniel

2015

A week after he'd arrived in the healer's village, Daniel still lay on the bed. The old man was standing over him. Daniel watched his lips move as he bent forward, his coloured beads dangling in front of his bare, ribbed chest. He was chanting to himself, preparing for the next stage of treatment. The right leg was splinted, and the healer appeared to be happy with its progress. But the complicated left leg was not improving as hoped.

"Tomorrow I will operate," the old man said, angling his head to get a different view of the broken limb. "I need to open you up and fix the bone myself."

His eyes met Daniel's.

"You will be brave," he said with confidence, and gently touched his patient's shoulder to show the consultation was over.

There was nothing to numb the pain, but Daniel was almost used to it, it felt like his brain no longer registered the suffering he experienced in other parts of his body. The shattered bone in his left leg was irreparable, the old man had decided, it would need to be removed and replaced. Four teenage boys, all a little younger than Daniel, had been positioned around the operating bed to hold him down. A nurse was kneeling by his head with water and a cool cloth. The old man murmured a prayer. He held a single, glinting blade in his hand, and sliced through the skin from the ankle to the knee. As Daniel's body tried to bolt upwards, the teenage boys did their job, each firmly holding a limb. Daniel pushed back for a moment, then submitted, closing his eyes. He lapsed in and out of consciousness. The surgery lasted an excruciating forty minutes. In a procedure the *mzee* had performed many times before, he removed the fragments of shattered bone and replaced them with a single piece of bamboo wood that his apprentice had cut to size. The new bone would grow around it, he had told Daniel. Once he was satisfied that the bamboo was in place and the leg would heal, he carefully sewed up the wound.

"Now the tree is part of you," the old man said.

Later, Daniel would look back at the months he spent in the healer's village with some affection. While borne out of extraordinary circumstances, his stay there was not untypical of any student's first year out of school – a new place and new experiences away from his family – but Daniel felt a weight of responsibility that set him apart from his peers. His first year of adulthood had transformed him from a carefree, talkative teenager to a young man troubled by guilt and pain.

After the operation, when he was satisfied that his son was out of danger, Daniel's father had headed back to Juba to settle the costs of the emergency transport and to raise more funds for his care. Two years into the war, the colonel's financial situation had taken a disastrous turn. Once comfortably off on his defence ministry salary, he had watched helplessly as the collapse of the South Sudanese pound and sky-rocketing inflation had devoured his savings. He had already been forced to borrow from relatives outside the country to pay for Daniel and his sister to finish school in Uganda. His houses in Bor had been destroyed. The Land Cruiser had gone and he had let his driver go. The gold he had bought for his young wife had been sold, along with the solar panels on the roof. Even Daniel's half-brother Akuei had been moved from Juba's prestigious American School to a cheaper alternative. Daniel's accident had dealt a blow to the family when it had been at its most vulnerable. He felt to blame. He had been nothing but a drain on his family, he thought as he lay recuperating under the shade of a tree. From now on he would strive to contribute. But first he had to get his legs to work.

"Today you are going to walk to that tree."

Daniel looked up. The old man had appeared at his bedside from nowhere. Daniel turned his head to where his healer was pointing – at a small scrubby tree about fifteen paces from his bed. It was a still November day; each morning was hotter than the last. Since his operation, Daniel had been cared for by the healer's apprentice who had carried out physiotherapy on Daniel's legs every day. The right one Daniel could bend and stretch with minimal pain, except for an arthritic ache from being bed-bound for so long. The left one was the difficult one. Still splinted, the incision had healed well. Two weeks after the surgery, under the instructions of the old man, the assistant had begun gentle massage and manipulation of the leg, and slowly Daniel had started to move it slightly himself. It hurt, certainly, but the overwhelming, savage pain he had endured for so long had subsided. His head felt clearer, clear enough for boredom to set in. Apart from several Bibles, there only seemed to be two books in this village, both belonging to the sister of his nurse. Well-thumbed survivors of several rainy seasons, the paperback volumes were in a state of near disintegration. Daniel had read them both, and then read them both again. They were voluptuous romances, with descriptions of speed boats, mansions and champagne parties. He found himself furtively rereading clichéd sex scenes with their metaphors of crashing waves and fiery eruptions. He would shift in his bed, thinking of Alice and her friends. He still longed for her, but now with a sense of shame. She hadn't chosen him, even when he was well and strong.

"First you will sit, then you will stand and then you will walk," the old man said again. The full team had gathered around the bed: the healer, his apprentice and the nurse who expertly turned him every few hours and tenderly washed him each evening. The old man had summoned two boys, both a little shorter than Daniel, to act as his crutches.

"*Mzee*, I can't walk!"

Daniel was already being pulled up to a sitting position. The nurse carefully swung his legs around so they hung from the bed. Daniel's knees were both bent for the first time since his accident. He felt a shock of pain.

"No! No!" he blurted, trying not to cry. "Please," he added softly. "I don't think I can walk."

The old man did not reply. Daniel was edged forwards on the bed, so his feet were planted on the ground. Without his weight on them, Daniel marvelled at the familiar feeling of the gritty earth under his bare feet. His back teeth bit down on the flesh inside his cheeks. He tried to control his quickening breath. The old man allowed him a few minutes to get used to the new position, to arch his back, roll his neck and wriggle his toes. This was enough, more than enough, but a slight nod from the healer was the signal for the two boys to take Daniel under each armpit and hoist him to standing. Daniel protested, but at the same time tried to straighten his long legs. He was standing, seeing the world from the top of his six-foot-five frame again. He shouted in Dinka, then laughed, and felt tears come to his eyes. He swallowed hard and the old man told him to take the first step.

He soon settled into a familiar routine. Each day he walked a little further, using wooden crutches carved from tree branches. He spent less time lying on his bed and was able to take himself to the toilet, shower in the washing hut, and eat sitting up. His diet was strictly controlled. For most people in the village dinner was a starchy maize or millet filler with beans, but Daniel's nurse prepared him only the food prescribed by the healer – bone marrow soup, chicken or pigeon with sorghum pancakes or rice, all more expensive than the local staples. The old man had saved his leg, even his life, but the final bill would come to thirty cows, and his father would be ruined.

Over the months of his recovery, Daniel joined the rhythm of village life in South Sudan. There were spells of boredom, of course, he missed his phone, which he'd left in Uganda. Maybe his sister had it, but it would be useless here anyway, with no signal and no power. He had plenty of time to think. He thought about his friends Joshua, Keno, Paul and Jimmy, about the night of the accident. He thought about the girls, Alice, Maureen, Michelle and Aisha, the party and the dancing. They had all been having so much fun. It had seemed like the beginning, but in fact it turned out to be the end.

Lying in bed at night, Daniel began to make plans for how he would redeem himself in the eyes of his friends and his father and bring honour back to the family. He could not expect his father to pay for his education any longer. But perhaps he could get a scholarship. Each year, the ten Senior Six students with the highest grades in each district in Uganda were awarded scholarships to study their chosen subject at Makerere University in Kampala. Daniel could not expect this, not least because he had not made the top ten in his school, let alone the district, and then there was the issue of not being Ugandan. But it had given him the idea. He knew nothing about university, what he could study or where. He had assumed before his accident that he would go to Juba, and he had planned to discuss with his father the possibility of studying economics. But now he would have to do it under his own steam. Sometimes he thought of outlandish plans and his head would buzz with excitement. He would go to America, a cousin on his mother's side already lived there, although he wasn't sure exactly where. He would go to Kenya – that's where he had been brought up, and some other kids had gone to study in Nairobi. Or Kampala – he could write and tell them about his accident, how he nearly died. Maybe they would take pity on him, decide to help him? Then his brain would slow down and reality would dawn. His teachers would not have many good words to say, and his exam results weren't exceptional. He was wasting his potential, they had told him, he needed to knuckle down, focus. But he had been lazy, complacent. And now it was too late.

CHAPTER 14

Lilian

September 2016

They made it to Ombachi with a couple of hours of daylight to spare. Hundreds of people had gathered in this one spot, under the trees by the primary school: old ladies with aching, swollen legs, hungry children, anxious men. They quickly got themselves organised: men went to gather firewood, some of the women fetched water, other started the fires. They would pool their resources – they would need to, to survive.

"Go on, go and play," Lilian gently encouraged Harmony. She had relaxed a little, there was a woman who had handed out cups of millet porridge to the children, and Harmony had finished the water she had collected in the jerrycan, gasping after each mouthful. Some kids had gathered under the school entrance, some playing with sticks, some just sitting on the steps, too exhausted to do much. Harmony wandered over shyly and soon seemed to be chatting to another boy a little older than him, and they started drawing patterns in the dust. Lilian offered her saucepan and some rice to the woman tending the fire. She enquired about cars, hoping they could leave in the morning. It should only be an hour's drive from here to Kaya on the border, it was just her and her son; how much would they charge?

The woman heard it before her. She flopped down suddenly like she had been deflated, her face was on the ground then her hands clawed at the dirt, as if she was trying to get herself into the earth. That was when Lilian heard the deadly whoosh of the artillery shells, she felt the air sucked from around her; a split second of silence and then a searing white light.

At first she thought she might be dead. She had been thrown across the ground, her eyes were burned shut. There was a vacuum of time, her head was empty, numb, perhaps her brain had been smashed out of her, there was no real thought. Time passed: it could have been a second, a minute, an hour. Lilian heard herself breathing. She dug her fingers in the dry earth and willed herself back to the present, to sit up, to move.

The volume turned up, louder and louder. She sat up, stood up, heard the screams, the wailing. She opened her eyes to the glare of fires burning the trees, the buildings, the cars. Madness whirled around her, people running, screaming. The air was thick with smoke. *Harmony! Harmony!* Lilian screamed, but couldn't hear her own voice. She ran in circles around the fires, crouching to touch a blackened body, running more, weaving around the horror scene in frenzied madness. The living were already leaving, fearing another attack. Cars revved away with doors open, other survivors just ran, scattering in all directions into the scrub.

"Come! Come now!" a man shouted, pulling Lilian's arm. "You must run!"

She went along, pulled by the stranger who tightly gripped her forearm. He had been right to tell her to run – as they stumbled along a path of dry leaves into the forest, another explosion nearly threw them to the ground. An unnatural glare lit up the dusk and the acrid smoke descended.

"No!" Lilian screamed. "No! Let me go! I need to go back! I need to find my son!"

She wrestled with the man, who kept hold of her arm as they both fell to the ground. Lilian struggled and kicked, trying to free herself. She lunged forward and tried to bite his shoulder, her mouth falling hard against bone.

"No!" she tried to scream. Her throat felt as sharp as razor blades; she could hear no sound. She tasted blood in her mouth. She lunged at the man again.

"Bitch! Stop it!" the man yelled. "Stop it!" His lip curled, he looked crazed. His shirt had been ripped off; his chest was heaving; his eye was bleeding. "You stupid bitch! We have to run, or we will die. Don't you understand? I'm trying to save you!"

They walked for hours through the night, a caravan of strangers – women, men, children, babies – who had all fled the bombing. They kept going until they came to the shelter of a mango tree. They dropped to the ground. The smallest infants, already limp bundles carried in arms and on shoulders, were placed down carefully after one of the women quickly swept the dirt ground with her hands. The older children sank gratefully onto the warm earth and fell unconscious, their dry mouths open and slack. Lilian lay down on her side and pulled her knees up to her chest. She had covered the tattered remnants of her primrose yellow dress with a *kitenge* that someone had passed to her. The shreds of the dress underneath were useless, but that was the last thing that Harmony had seen his mother wearing. When he started to search for her, she thought, if he had to describe her to someone, he would remember the dress, so she would not take it off, not until she had found him again. Her son had been wearing his blue shorts and blue-and-red striped T-shirt. Was he wearing them now? Where was he? Was he trying to sleep too, lying down with a group of strangers?

She lay behind a little girl a few years older than Harmony, probably about nine. She didn't know her; she didn't know anyone in the group. There had been no time for talking, but the others seemed to understand that Lilian had not been travelling alone before the attack. They helped her take sips of water in the darkness when they got to the stream. Lying still now, Lilian listened to the sleeping girl's murmurs; she watched her tiny ribcage gently rise and fall. She wanted to reach out and place her hand on the girl's back. That's what she did with Harmony, and they would both drift off to sleep together, breathing in unison.

But Lilian could not sleep on this night. She lay awake, with the glassy, open eyes of a doll. She turned her neck to watch the dawn sky turn to violet through the canopy of leaves. Was Harmony looking up at it too? She should never have let him go and play, she should have stayed with him, holding his hand. She deserved the agony she felt, the stabbing pains in her heart, the nausea rising in her windpipe. She would not eat until she found him. She would starve herself, but when she found him again she would cook him his *posho* and beans, then she would kill a chicken for him, and they would eat it together.

What should have been a two- or three-day walk to the Ugandan border turned into an epic journey of endurance that Lilian bore without complaint. If anything, the pain felt appropriate to her, she deserved it. She even wondered, when she was walking, whether the more she suffered the more likely she was to see Harmony again.

The road to Kaya, the fastest route to Uganda, was unsafe. On the second day they had encountered a group of terrified retreating civilians, staggering up the road towards them. They had started off as nine, but they had been ambushed by rebel fighters who had robbed them, accused the three men in their group of being deserters, and slaughtered them on the spot with their machetes. They wouldn't waste bullets on cowards, the rebels had said. The bodies were left on the side of the road to rot in the sun, then they gang-raped the women, including a twelve-year-old girl, forcing the two young boys to watch. When they had finished, they ordered the depleted group back up the road towards Yei, knowing that if government soldiers came upon them the routine would be repeated.

The six survivors joined Lilian's weary band and, like her, became quiet, compliant followers, leaving all decision-making to the two men and one woman who had emerged as natural leaders. If the Kaya road was impassable, they would have to head west, through the bush to Congo, one of the men had said. He had been there before, when he was driving petrol tankers, but he hadn't been on foot. He tried to laugh. This would be hard, at least a week's walk to Congo, then they would try to get themselves down to Koboko on the Ugandan border. The Congolese were crazy, the man had said, but they won't try to hurt us. It's the only way.

They were constantly on the move, sleeping for two or three hours at a time and then heading on. Sometimes Lilian fell into a heavy sleep within seconds of lying down and would awake disorientated and remorseful if she had not dreamt about Harmony. Most of her waking hours she was thinking of him, from his babyhood to now, talking to him, replaying scenes in her head and desperately trying to scrape up fresh memories of their six years together. Like her, everyone in the group seemed to have retreated into themselves, conserving energy, barely speaking, except to chivvy along their shrunken, exhausted children. Lilian listened to their quiet, thin cries in the night and wondered if anyone was listening out for Harmony.

After days and nights that Lilian could not count they crossed into Congo. There was no border post but they noticed subtle changes in the landscape and then they saw the houses that were different from theirs and the sign by the church that they could not read. At the end of that day, two women had approached with stiff braids spiking from their heads like antennae, offering coconuts from a wicker basket. When the refugees turned up their palms to show they had nothing, the women conferred, cut open half a dozen shells with their *pangas* and handed out the brown husks to the children, who lifted them to their ravenous mouths and tipped them up for the warm, sweet juice.

They all felt safer in Congo, seeking out churches at night where they could rest nearby, and allowing themselves longer stretches of sleep. To the locals they were a curiosity, and despite the lack of a common language there was an understanding of the travellers' plight. These borderlands were scarred by conflict: when one area had been at peace, another was at war. While the refugees felt no hostility here, they were resolved to reach Uganda. Congo was unfamiliar, and in times of trouble it was Uganda that had been the place of refuge for the South Sudanese; in turn they had hosted plenty of Ugandan refugees when their neighbours had been in turmoil. They were brothers, they shared traditions, languages and a way of life that stretched back way before any of these borders had been drawn. What's more, it was in Uganda that the United Nations would be waiting for them, with shelter and food for their children.

They walked for more than a week. Their legs were pitted with scabbed and raw scratches, their feet blistered and bleeding. Pain was something they observed now, rather than felt. Their clothes were rags, their hair was red from the dust. Each morning, they smeared ash from the fire's embers on their faces to reflect the glaring midday sun. By evening, the children stared at the adults, shocked at the creatures their parents had become.

On one night, just one or two days away from the Ugandan border, Lilian lay in absolute darkness, her throat so parched she could barely swallow and a dull ache in her belly. A black thought had stalked her through this whole journey, circling like a vulture. Each time she pushed it back, banishing it to that place in her head that was the repository of all things bad in her life – her mother leaving, her husband's death. It was somewhere Lilian never went; that was how she kept going. Even through this painful trek she held out hope, pushing herself, starving herself, telling herself that with each step she was moving towards Harmony, not away from him. But on that night, lying once again on the hard ground, Lilian forced herself to reconstruct the twilight hour when her son was lost.

She had sent him over to the school steps to play with the others. He had been anxious about leaving her side, but she told him to go, and he would never disobey her. Harmony was still a young boy but so sharp; he understood everything. Since his father died he had been watchful around her, anticipating her needs. When she used to wash the clothes she would wring out the water and he would stand by to take each piece and hang it carefully on the line. When it was time to make the fire he would run to collect the kindling without being asked. When she was tired he would fetch the water himself, staggering back with a half-filled container. One time he poured some water into a bowl and gently washed her feet. They would eat together, read Lilian's schoolbooks together, fall asleep together. She had never told Harmony she loved him; their bond was unspoken.

Back to that day. The last time she saw him he was playing

with the other children in front of the school. She was cooking with that woman; why had she let him go from her side? He had smiled at her, she remembered. How long was it, between the time she looked over to see him and the explosion? She had been busy with the cooking, talking to that woman, trying to make plans, how to move on.

Everything looked different after the attack. Everything was on fire. She didn't know which way she was facing, which direction the school was in. She couldn't find the school or any of the children. Had she been looking in the right place? There were fires everywhere, black smoke and bodies. Why didn't she spend more time looking for him? Why did she run away? Lying on the ground in the dark, Lilian clawed at her arms with her brittle broken nails. She scratched and scratched until she drew blood. There was only one reason why she had left him. She knew why she had left her only son. Because he was dead.

The next morning, they kept on through the forest, walking through patterns of light and shade. One of the children spotted it first – a papaya tree! The little girl ran up to it, strangely silent; the children were all mute now. The others followed, wordlessly searching on the ground for a stick long and strong enough to shake down the unripe fruit. One of the men found one and set about beating the branches while two of the children tried desperately to climb the tree, which they would have conquered with ease when they were healthy. In half an hour they had plucked off most of the pale green fruit, each one barely the size of a chicken's egg. They bit through the hard skin to the white flesh beneath.

Lilian grabbed two in each hand and started gnawing on the unripe fruit, almost choking as she tried to swallow the bitter, sinewy flesh. The others watched her, surprised. They continued walking and Lilian kept on, spitting bits of skin to the ground as she searched for something to satisfy her desperate hunger. Two women behind her muttered their approval. This was the first time they had seen her eat. They thought she might be healing, trying to get her strength up. It was a hopeful sign, they thought.

They were wrong. The truth was Lilian had lost all hope. She felt no more pain, in fact, she felt a strange sense of elation. She was walking faster than ever on her bare, blistered feet, and constantly scavenging for food – green shoots, whole birds' eggs, insects, anything she could find. She ate ravenously. She didn't bother to share it. She was breaking her own rules now because nothing mattered any more. Lilian saw herself as just another animal, driven to survive, her heart empty and her humanity gone.

CHAPTER 15

Veronica

2015–2016

Baby Sunday was mellow and compliant. Veronica breastfed her and she was growing well. The baby's first smile came when she was nearly three months old; she was lying on her back on their bare foam mattress, wriggling her limbs in the air as Veronica gently tickled her tummy. Soon after that, Sunday learned how to suck her thumb and settle herself to sleep.

"You used to do that," Veronica's mother would say, almost smiling, when the baby reached each milestone, and Veronica would question her more. "At what age did I walk? What was my first word?" Since giving birth, Veronica would think wistfully about her own childhood in jumbled, blurry images, as if she was looking back on it from a great age. She liked to remember the time when her father was there and he would sing her and her brothers to sleep in the velvety rural night. She liked to remember the afternoons she spent with her friends under the big tree near their school in Bentiu, their games and their jokes that only they understood. In a present that seemed so painful, Veronica romanticised the past, and in her bleakest moments she would delve into it for comfort. Motherhood was not the problem. Her love for her daughter had come easily and the demands of her new role, the nursing, burping and bathing, didn't bother her. What caused that sickening, hollowed-out feeling that gnawed at her day and night and refused to leave was her yearning for Jackson.

Just before Christmas, when Sunday was four months old, Veronica's mother finally agreed that Jackson could meet his baby daughter. There had been a brief exchange between the two families when Veronica's pregnancy became evident. Usually, in such circumstances, the young couple would be forced to marry, no matter their age. But in a single, frosty meeting, Veronica's mother and Jackson's aunt failed to find a consensus that might have paved the way for a hasty wedding before the birth. Jackson's aunt made it clear that no bride price would be paid for Veronica, as was the tradition in South Sudan. Given her beauty, her family would have hoped to have scooped a fair number of cows for Veronica, but now she was sullied goods, she was worthless – Jackson's aunt had made that plain. In those circumstances, the only course of action was to cut ties, and Veronica's mother had informed her daughter she was not to meet her boyfriend ever again.

But after Sunday's birth, Jackson had begged to see the baby. He made his entreaties formally, respectfully, in neat, handwritten notes addressed to Veronica's mother that he passed to Santino at school. He never turned up at the house, or even hung around the neighbourhood in the hope of seeing them. Veronica tearfully begged her mother to let him come, just to see the baby, and eventually, grudgingly, she agreed. Santino was dispatched to Jackson's house and within thirty minutes they were both back again, out of breath; Jackson had run the half a kilometre back, with Santino jogging behind.

Veronica's heart pounded when she saw her boyfriend for the first time in more than half a year. She couldn't contain her smile; she was almost giggling. She didn't care what her mother thought. Jackson was smiling too; a line of sweat trickled from his hairline in front of his ear. He sat down on one of their two plastic chairs, as indicated by Veronica's mother, who stood on watching, her arms folded, her mouth set in a line.

"This is Sunday," said Veronica gently, tugging back the swaddling blanket from around the baby's chin to reveal her full, round face. Sunday was quiet, her clear, wet eyes staring up, unfocused, to the tin roof. "Would you like to hold her?"

Jackson leaned forward to take hold of the bundle. As he took his baby daughter in his arms for the first time, he reached for Veronica's hand under the blanket and gently squeezed it. Her mother may have seen, but to them the woman was invisible. The young parents sat, in wonderment, staring at the child they had created.

Sunday's eyes widened as her father's face came into focus for the first time. Jackson gazed at her, absorbing every feature, her lashes, her tiny ears, nose, perfect lips. He laughed with joy.

He looked up at Veronica, gently shaking his head. "She is beautiful," he whispered.

After that, there was no way the couple could stay apart. They were still in love, and their powerful devotion to Sunday only made those feelings stronger. Stealthily, they began to see each other again. With Santino acting as go-between, Veronica would let Jackson know when she would be going to the market, Sunday always in a sling on her back. Jackson would sneak out of school to meet her for a few stolen minutes. Then they grew bolder. Jackson could not visit her house; it was too much of a risk, the neighbours would be quick to report his presence to Veronica's mother. But when her mother was at work, Veronica began sneaking to Jackson's house, when his aunt was at her chapati stall. He had to miss class, against his better judgement, but the lure of seeing Veronica and his baby daughter was too strong. For a few hours each week, the young couple would be reunited in the dark, windowless house where Sunday was conceived.

Sunday was walking and starting to babble when the war caught up with Veronica again. It was early evening and she was in the house with her mother, younger sister and little daughter when they heard shooting. Quickly, they shut the door and barricaded themselves in by pushing the bed against it. The boys had been at the base playing football. There was no way to contact them. Veronica and her mother stayed inside all night, not daring to come out, even after the shooting died down. In the morning, they peered out of the door. Their neighbours were still sheltering indoors, but Riek's men were about. It looked like they were gathering at the barracks up the track. Veronica and her mother shut the door and locked it again. Sunday was crying. There was still no sign of Santino and Simon. Veronica and her mother dipped their heads and murmured prayers for them, her mother slipping plastic rosary beads through her fingers. Silently, Veronica prayed for Jackson too.

The next morning was quiet and Veronica was starting to think it was over, a one-off. But then they heard thunder in the sky and felt the ground shaking beneath them.

"Mummy, what's happening?"

It was unfortunate that they lived so close to Riek's base in Gudele. A peace agreement had fallen apart and Salva and Riek had kicked off another battle in the centre of Juba. Riek's bodyguards had rushed him back to the protection of his house and Salva had ordered that he be hunted down. Helicopter gunships clattered in the sky; rockets pulverised the ground around them. The family's shack trembled with each detonation; they could hear shouts and screams and they could smell explosives and burning.

When the evening rain came the family dashed to Saint Theresa's cathedral, almost a mile away on the main road. The UN compound was too far; the church had no protection except for the brick wall surrounding it, but they hoped they would be safe. Veronica carried Sunday and her mother ran with Amani. That night they slept side by side on the stone floor. In the morning, Veronica woke up to find her mother's little cloth purse with a few crumpled, almost valueless notes inside had been tucked under her shoulder. Her mother was not there. Veronica picked up Sunday and with her sister she searched the church, the vestry, the grounds, the latrine block. Hundreds of people had come to seek sanctuary at the cathedral, so it would have been easy to miss her, but after an hour of searching Veronica slumped down on the ground in despair.

The woman who ran the grocery store stood over her. She had never been kind to them.

"I saw her go. She's run off with Riek's people," the woman said with a smirk.

Veronica remained impassive, as if she hadn't heard, and turned her head away. The woman tutted and moved off. Veronica buried her face in her hands and cried. Her toddler daughter leaned against her.

Veronica's mother had been with soldiers all her life and saw herself as one of them. She cooked for them, and she knew how to handle a Kalashnikov too. She didn't really enjoy civilian life, Veronica knew that. So she'd gone back to join the rebels again, Riek's breakaway army. Although it was dangerous, crazy, although she was abandoning her children and her little granddaughter, ditching all her responsibilities, the pull was too strong. She wanted to fight. As her family slept, she had slipped out of the cathedral, into the warring city, dashed back to her house, grabbed a few clothes and gone straight up to Riek's base. They knew her; she was one of them. Under attack, Riek and his men fled the city that night and Veronica's mother was with them.

There was still shooting in the city, and the evacuees in the church grounds were getting into groups and leaving. They were going to the border, Veronica heard. She didn't know where that was or what it meant – whether it was Juba or somewhere else. She wished Jackson was with her – he would know what to do.

She latched on to one group, walking with her sister by her side and Sunday in her arms. They walked through the city. It was empty, tense, strewn with the debris of fighting just like that day they had walked out of the UN base. They stayed together and made it as far as the Nimule road on the edge of town. There were metal-spiked barriers on the ground to stop cars going further, and swarms of soldiers questioning everyone who was trying to leave. Veronica could hear shouting ahead, men scuffling, a gunshot. Then one of the women with her must have said something wrong. A soldier in camouflage fatigues and black boots shot the woman in the chest, right there, on the side of the road, in front of them all. Her body crumpled to the ground and blood spread like a flower in the dirt. Veronica's little sister was screaming but the soldier just smiled at them, as if it hadn't happened. His right hand was bleeding.

"Get in," he ordered. "Get in the pickup. I will take you to the border."

Veronica's body was tense, she was ready to bolt. The soldier was still holding his rifle. How easily he had shot it. He didn't seem to notice his own wound; he hadn't tried to stop the bleeding. Veronica had no choice. She climbed into the pickup's cab first so she would be sitting next to him. She had to lean out to lift Amani and Sunday in next to her.

Her job now was to protect the girls. A wooden cross and a small, laminated photo of Salva Kiir in his cowboy hat hung from the rear-view mirror. She pulled the door shut and the soldier turned the ignition key awkwardly with his good left hand. His wounded arm sat limply in his lap as the truck roared to life.

CHAPTER 16

Lilian

October 2016

Once she crossed the border from Congo into Uganda, Lilian left the group – with whom she had shared the most challenging episode of her life – with a murmur of thanks and barely a backwards glance. She knew where she would go first. She found the road to Koboko, and set out along its dusty edge, still in the remnants of her once yellow dress, covered with the filthy *kitenge.* Minibuses and lorries plying cross-border trade thundered past, throwing up billows of red dust which landed softly upon her. Five miles from town, a *matatu* pulled up, looking for a last fare, but when the conductor got a closer look at Lilian – barefoot, dirty and half starved – he yanked the sliding door shut and the bus accelerated off again.

In the mess of South Sudan's old war Lilian's mother had ended up on the Ugandan side of the border, in the town of

Koboko, scratching through her allotted time on earth with so little margin that not even family life could be maintained. Lilian was barely an adult when her mother took off for the promise of some kind of work, and the two had vaguely kept in touch, when someone went to sell something over the border or by message sent from a neighbour's mobile phone in South Sudan to another neighbour's phone in Uganda. Lilian had let her mother know when she married Samuel and when Harmony was born, and her mother had congratulated her but said she was sorry, she had no money to come home to meet the new family.

It was late by the time Lilian walked into town. The evening brick fires glowed in the darkness. Koboko was a scrappy frontier town, its main landmark a giant mobile phone mast tethered to the ground by metal cables. It had been up for about five years, the flashing red beacon at its peak now a feature in the night sky as familiar to residents as the moon and stars. Around a centre of concrete shops and lockups with sacks of grain or crates of soft drinks and beer, the town was encircled by a scattering of square mud houses. It took just a few enquiries for Lilian to find the right place, and when she got to the house, dimly lit by a kerosene lamp, she softly announced her arrival through the doorway. Her mother emerged, saw Lilian and stepped back with an appalled look of recognition. They stood staring at each other, Lilian reacquainting herself with her mother's comfortless face and her mother absorbing Lilian's feral appearance.

"Where is the boy?" her mother asked at last.

"He is gone. I lost him," Lilian said flatly.

Lilian saw a flicker of relief in her mother's eyes. It was a beat, a microsecond, almost imperceptible. But Lilian was sure she had seen it. After a momentary pause, her mother clasped her hands to her chest, opened her mouth in horror and began exclaiming at a volume that the neighbours could not but hear. "The boy, oh the boy!" she cried. "Oh, my grandson! My grandson! May the Lord have mercy!"

Lilian looked impassive, but heat seared up through her body and sirens blared in her ears. She accepted her mother's invitation to enter the dingy house and she sat down on a wooden stool, gripping its edges. She didn't speak. She stared ahead. In her mind she was battering her mother, slapping her with her hands, scratching her with her fingernails, kicking her, screaming at her. She understood of course – her mother was painfully poor: she could only think about herself.

After that, she knew she would not stay long. Her mother was as kind as she could be. She fetched Lilian a bucket of water and gave her soap to clean off the fourteen days of horror. She fed her. She combed and braided her daughter's hair for the first time since Lilian was a child. She gave her a dress, some underwear, trying not to look too pained as she handed over the sorry garments. But her mother could not share her life with her, and when Lilian got up one morning and said she was heading for Bidi Bidi, the refugee settlement where she would at least be fed, her mother seemed grateful to pack her off.

She had no money to offer for the journey, but gave her daughter something much more precious: a photograph of Harmony and Lilian, a proper portrait taken in a studio in Yei that Lilian had saved up for when Harmony turned five.

Elegant in a black skirt and pink blouse, Lilian sits with her legs crossed on the photographer's chair, her arm around Harmony who stands, chest out, in a striped T-shirt, long trousers and new, clean sandals. Lilian had loved that picture and had paid for an extra print to send to her mother.

She tucked the photo inside her dress and held her hand against it as she walked through her tears towards the main road.

PART 2

The camp is called Bidi Bidi. The soil is thin and stony and the sun is harsh. No one else has ever wanted to live on this unyielding, windswept land, too far from the river, exposed and undefined. Just a hundred miles to the south, the waters of the White Nile thunder over the Murchison Falls and a lush wildlife reserve draws safari tourists to spot elephants, lions and buffalo. Bidi Bidi, a patchy forest inhabited by snakes and scorpions, offers no such attractions. But in the space of just a few months it has become a sanctuary for hundreds of thousands of people fleeing South Sudan's civil war, a generation that should have been the first to grow up in a new, hopeful nation. The war has robbed them of that chance. Stories like the one of the fourteen-year-old boy who buried his own family are replicated here, thousands of times over.

Technically, it's not a camp, it's a settlement. The difference is the settlement has no fences around it; everyone is free to come and go, although most are too poor to go anywhere. Under a refugee policy hailed as one of the most compassionate in the world, Uganda has allocated each family a plot to cultivate, even though the refugees complain the soil is poor and they have no seeds or tools. They are free to work, but there are few jobs. The United Nations and aid agencies like Save the Children and World Vision ensure the refugees are fed, watered and sheltered. They distribute monthly rations of maize, sorghum, vegetable oil, beans and salt. As stick-and-plastic shelters colonise the gentle rises of forest and scrub, the agencies drill boreholes to tap underground water reserves and build tanks set on high wooden platforms and a network of water pipes to supply each of the new administration zones.

Bidi Bidi is not a cash-rich economy; the refugees' purchasing power is feeble to non-existent; many have not handled cash since leaving South Sudan – for months or even years. Food is provided to every resident who has registered and holds a ration card. Water has been made available across the scrubby, undulating wastes of the settlement through a Herculean project overseen by the United Nations. Aid agencies have helped refugees to build their shelters, prioritising the most vulnerable: the elderly, the disabled and the mentally ill. Schools have been built and the wood and tarpaulin structures of the early days replaced with permanent, concrete buildings, while small health centres provide basic medicines, ante-natal care and vaccines for children.

All in all, it is an astonishing achievement; the basic needs of a new population the size of a small city have been met within a matter of months – nearly every refugee has shelter, food and water. But there is no margin for any kind of extras. Items such as soap for washing clothes, plastic sandals for children, coveted school uniforms or solar lamps have become luxuries. Each of the settlement's five zones is sub-divided into so-called villages that are merely clusters of houses, initially without shops or markets. It isn't a great place to start a business, but slowly, inevitably, an economy has started to grow. Along tracks cut by Caterpillar diggers, covered wooden stalls have appeared, selling second-hand clothes, packets of washing powder, sachets of sweet cherry or mango concentrate to mix with water, malt biscuits, tomatoes and onions. There are bicycle repair shops, hair salons and kiosks selling pay-as-you-go top-ups for the minority who own mobile phones.

Base camp is in Zone One, the first area to be populated when the refugees started arriving. UN Land Cruisers roar up and down the pitted track to the gates of the dusty compound. Inside are rows of air-conditioned shipping containers repurposed as offices, a white-washed, concrete toilet block off in the far corner, and a cafe selling bottled water, soft drinks, coffee and chapatis for the camp staff. In the middle is a meeting hall made of tarpaulin strung over a wooden frame. The parking area is full of NGO-branded vehicles – World Vision, Oxfam, Care, the International Rescue Committee. These and a dozen more aid agencies are working here, dividing up the tasks of providing services in the settlement between them.

"Good morning, brothers and sisters!"

Camp commander Robert Baryamwesiga – a stocky, can-do

man in a khaki photographer's vest and desert boots – opens the coordination meeting to which each agency has dispatched their representatives. More than a hundred aid workers are packed onto wooden benches, all sporting their organisation's T-shirts or hi-viz vests. They are mostly Ugandans: as part of the government's deal with the United Nations to host the refugees, Uganda has secured an agreement stipulating that nearly all aid workers employed to run the emergency response would be locals. It's an African-led mission, quickly regarded as successful, both for the refugees and for the local population. Every dollar of aid money spent is split between incomers and residents, with seventy cents going to refugees and thirty cents going to help the local community, who benefit from road construction, water points, schools and medical centres.

The reasons for the community's acceptance of refugees on such a huge scale runs deeper than the mere fringe benefits, however. They know these people. Some of the new arrivals are returning refugees, they have lived in Uganda before, and many have been educated there. In turn, northern Uganda's own insurgency had once pushed many Ugandans north, across the border, and in peacetime Ugandans, with higher levels of education, had crossed the border to take up jobs as teachers, engineers and medics. There are ties of family, business and culture – a reservoir of admiration for the other. The Uganda–South Sudan border, less than a century old, does not have the same significance on the ground as the solid line on the map implies. People have moved back and forth freely for centuries, they are brothers – many of whom share the same languages and traditions.

But of course there are tensions, rivalries and violence. The forced displacement of a quarter of South Sudan's population has created the world's fastest moving and biggest refugee flow, a movement on a biblical scale that cannot not be without problems. There are disputes over resources, especially trees, of which there are too few. While the host community's villages are built around the sturdy mango or neem trees, the newcomers live in an exposed landscape of spiky desert bushes which offer little shade or protection. Women walk miles in search of firewood, each week further and further as resources are quickly depleted. Everyone in the camp knows a woman who has been raped when out looking for firewood; it is such a common occurrence that few of the attacks are reported. Some local people complain that the refugees are treated better than them, while refugees say they are not given police protection, proper education or enough food. In Kampala, Ugandan government officials responsible for refugees' care are accused of inflating their numbers in order to embezzle some of the aid funds.

In the meeting tent, aid workers step up to the microphone to deliver updates on construction, child protection, sanitation and health. The meeting stretches into its third hour and individually wrapped biscuits and bottles of water and soda are passed around. When the reports are complete, the commander takes back the microphone and names and shames the humanitarian agencies that he says are not carrying out their duties to his satisfaction.

"People are suffering!" he cries. The aid workers look contritely at their flip-flopped feet.

There are many problems in the camp, the commander notes, but as he sees it, there is one big one, one they must tackle together.

"If you are a child of sixteen and you are forced to watch as the soldiers rape your mother, how do you feel?" he asks. "We must help people heal inside. We must give hope for tomorrow, or they will see no reason in living."

It's getting unbearably hot in the airless tent but the commander, pacing the front with evangelical energy, wants to hammer the point home.

"It is not enough to save lives!" he says. "What is it not enough to do?" His rising inflection demands a response.

"Save lives," the aid workers mumble in an unconvincing chorus.

"That's right, it is not enough to save lives! What is the purpose of saving lives if we can't sustain them?" he enquires, rhetorically this time. "Once we have saved lives we must nurture lives. Even if you have lost everything, your life can still be worth living."

The aid workers nod their understanding. The meeting is over. They rise from their benches, roll their necks, stretch their arms and file out into the glare and dust.

CHAPTER 17

Daniel

October 2016

At the camp, Daniel is the only man in the queue at the water tap. The women around him giggle and pinch him; they are amused, but his presence also makes them feel uneasy. Back in South Sudan, men don't fetch water, even for their own showers. They don't weed the fields or do any of the menial tasks that women could do. They do not separate the grain, wash the clothes, look for firewood or do the cooking. There are strict rules. A married man will only eat a meal that has been prepared by his wife. If his wife is sick or indisposed, and he doesn't have other wives as backup, he will go hungry. But Daniel is different. By the age of nineteen, he has lived in three countries. He's been on a football tour to Tanzania and been educated at a Ugandan boarding school. He doesn't think of himself as a typical refugee, corralled into a camp. He fetches his own water when he wants to wash; he even cleans his mother's and sister's clothes when he is doing his own.

Walking back towards their new home, Daniel struggles to balance the container on his head. Toweringly tall, he isn't cut out for this. Precious water sloshes onto his T-shirt. Two barefooted girls pad swiftly by despite the burden of heavy water pots. They giggle, casting glances up at him but keeping their heads dead still, needing just the light touch of their fingers to keep their containers in place. Daniel, his head equally fixed, can't look down at them, but he can hear their laughter. He really doesn't care, he wants them to think of him as different, because he *is* different, and that's why he won't be stuck in this place for long.

This is the second refugee camp Daniel has lived in. When he was a toddler, his father went to fight in the bush and didn't return. There was no word, no contact, and soon, no money. His mother took Daniel and his baby sister to Kakuma, the scorched, windswept camp across the border in Kenya. How else could they survive? Two more years went by with no word from the colonel or news of his fate, and the family officially declared him dead. After a suitable period of mourning, a Dinka tradition had to be upheld: a brother of the deceased should ensure the continuation of his lineage. The colonel already had nine children by three marriages, but his newest wife, Daniel's mother, was still young and such a fine man deserved an even greater legacy. So on moonless nights when the camp was dark, Daniel's uncle would visit his mother in their UN tent in Kakuma, an arrangement his uncle's own wife had no choice but to accept. This way,

Daniel acquired two more siblings, regarded by the family as belonging to his late father.

As Daniel grew older and went to school he began to learn about other places in the world, all of them, he slowly discovered, better than Kakuma. The camp was set in the arid pastoral lands of northern Kenya that had for centuries been home to a smattering of cattle herders. Now it housed hundreds of thousands of people from Sudan, Somalia and Ethiopia. Basic rations ensured survival. The camp was a social leveller; Daniel's mother's status as the widow of a war hero and the daughter of a village chief meant little here. For much of her time in Kakuma she was breastfeeding one of her infants, and until they could walk they would be strapped to her back while she squatted to cook or walked from the water-pump with her chin high and a jerrycan on her head. There were families who spent years, even decades, there. But it always felt like an artificial home, a dusty, bleak limbo-land. Even as a youngster, Daniel understood that, in a refugee camp, escape was the only future.

One blisteringly hot Saturday when Daniel was almost nine, he and his friends were playing football in the alley and his mother had half an eye on her youngest children playing outside the tent, when a Kenyan camp worker, his orange vest marking out his status, rounded the corner, looking around, looking for someone. He stooped to speak to Daniel's mother, who was washing clothes. She looked up, met his eyes and listened, her mouth slightly open. Daniel kicked the football away, went over to his mother, and stood nearby, listening.

His mother left her washing in the soapy water, wiped her

hands on the front of her skirt and shouted to a neighbour to watch the children. There was a radio call for her at the Red Cross office in the camp. This was unusual. Daniel had seen others summoned to receive calls, but never his mother. She followed the aid worker to the huge Red Cross tent in the next block, her eyes fixed on the logo on the back of his vest. Daniel trailed behind her; she hadn't said he couldn't.

"Call from Narus! Martha Adut Deng, wife of Colonel Deng Phillips Bol!" Daniel watched his mother jump up, startled, from the white plastic chair where she had been told to sit. She seemed to stumble towards the radio operator. "Caller, you can speak," the operator instructed. "Your wife is here."

His mother stared at the microphone on the table in front of her. Daniel had never seen her look so confused, so alone. Then a crackle on the line and a commanding voice broke through the static. "Adut! I have found you!" A boom of laughter down the line. "How are you? How are the children?"

His mother opened her mouth to speak, and closed it again. Daniel felt dizzy, the blood had drained from his head.

His father, his dead father, was speaking here on the radio.

A decade later and Daniel is back in a refugee camp. When the war erupted in Juba again, Daniel's father couldn't help. He could no longer commandeer trucks and boats to help his son escape. His father's house is gone, his Land Cruiser is gone, all his savings are gone. He can no longer support his four wives. He has retreated to the bush, commanding a unit of soldiers in a remote part of Jonglei State. Daniel left Juba on a convoy of buses and found his mother, sister and little brothers in Uganda, with nothing. His little sister Tabitha had dropped out of school. There was no choice but to head to the refugee settlements that had mushroomed across the rocky hunting grounds between Arua and the Nile. Being a refugee in Uganda has advantages over Kenya; the family has a little piece of land on which to build their own house. But almost immediately, Daniel started to feel the drain of refugee life. Some people adapt easily to the dependency, they feel unburdened by the removal of choices. Daniel has watched his mother and sister settle in without complaint. They have succumbed to the system, they embrace it even – queuing to register, queuing for cooking utensils, queuing for food, queuing for water. They are so accepting, and it annoys him. He feels annoyed for weeks and his mother chides him for his bad temper. He's nearly twenty, but still playing the part of a truculent teenager: grumpy, bored and monosyllabic. His days are spent sitting outside their *tukul*, strumming out repetitive, dreary ballads on his guitar.

He watches his horizons narrow. It's a physical sensation, as if he is slowly losing his sight. He's been to one of the best schools in northern Uganda. Although he could have studied harder, he's had a much better education than most of the young people in the camp. His aspirations have always been vague, but at school he'd had a sense that anything was possible. He should be at university, not mouldering in this no-man's-land. His school-friends are all studying – in Gulu, Kampala and Mbarara. Once or twice, Daniel is able to buy some airtime at the cafe near the UN's basecamp. He goes onto Facebook to see how his friends have moved on: Keno in his university dormitory, a selfie of Paul in a white coat and safety glasses – he is training to be a medical technician. Josh is on a field trip to a sugar factory, wearing a hard hat and posing for the camera with peace signs. Daniel clicks on the pictures, zooms in for detail. He stares at them until his internet time runs out.

CHAPTER 18

Veronica

December 2016

Veronica has been in Bidi Bidi for five months. On arrival, she told the registration people her age – she was almost seventeen – and the fact that she was in sole charge of her nearly two-year-old daughter and ten-year-old sister. These responsibilities didn't qualify her for any extra help, however, there are plenty of parentless children – known as unaccompanied minors – arriving in the camp every day. Many of them, like Veronica, are looking after younger children. Veronica has been given blankets, some cooking utensils and ration cards to collect food. She has a small plot of land in Zone One, Village Eleven, where the soil is as dry as dust.

Like everyone else, the family starts off under a shelter of sticks and tarpaulin, sleeping on the bare ground, even through the short rains. Life is miserable, almost unbearable.

The three girls are hungry and wet, never comfortable. When Amani, her little sister, uses up the last of her energy to have a tantrum one night, kicking down a pole that holds up their tent, Veronica slaps her, hard, with an anger that now lives close to the surface. Her sister is quiet after that, for weeks, and Veronica feels sorry for her. The little girl has lice in her hair, her skin is grey and dirty and she scratches compulsively at the mosquito bites on her arms and legs. She wears a filthy vest and denim shorts with a ripped black skirt on top, a combination which keeps her just about decent.

Veronica seems to bear the discomfort, the hunger and the responsibility of life as a refugee with stoicism. She gets up, sweeps around the shelter, fetches water, builds the fire. She makes sense of the food distribution system, although no one has explained it to her, and queues up on the correct day to receive the rations she is due. Then she sells just enough maize to pay for the grinding of the rest of the grain. She needs it to be smooth to make the baby's porridge. The next month she sells more; they need soap to wash their clothes and bodies. On the third month she parts with even a little more, this time to buy millet because the maize does not agree with the toddler's stomach. These precise calibrations keep them alive. Veronica does not spend time wishing for things like food and clothes. She tries to be tough; she is often sharp with the children. But, despite her capable exterior, she is missing Jackson with the fervour of the teenager she is. At night, when the little girls are asleep, she turns her back on them, closes her eyes and relives the times she spent with him as if she is watching a film. She longs for him, obsesses about him, imagines him. She envisages him walking into the settlement, coming to her tent, surprising her. She imagines how she will be when she sees him, how she would apologise for the surroundings, how he would pick up little Sunday and they would all laugh together. He would tell her what he had been doing these past months, that he has missed her so much and that he has decided they must be together. Then she would tell him the news she hasn't been able to tell anyone else: she is pregnant again.

It's December, hot and dry, and the camp's residents are trying to upgrade their shelters to more durable mud-and-thatch homes before the long rains come. Wilbur is Veronica's neighbour in Village Eleven. Back at home, it would have been unlikely their paths would have crossed. Wilbur is a Pentecostal preacher in his thirties with a wife and two young children. While Veronica comes from a military family, Wilbur has gone to great lengths to avoid being sucked into one of South Sudan's many militia groups. He is a fervent believer in Jesus; Veronica would say she is too, but in reality she has never had the time nor the education to really consider her Catholic faith in any depth. They are from different tribes; she a Nuer, he a Kakwa. But now here they are, living side by side.

Wilbur has made all the necessary and painful self-sacrifices to scrape together the funds to build a one-roomed weatherproof house for his wife Christine, their daughter Blessing and baby son Given. From her next-door plot, Veronica watches them mark out the footprint of their new home with sticks before laying rows of kiln-fired bricks. Wilbur has sold the bicycle he wheeled from South Sudan to pay for the bricks and fasted for a month to buy the grass for the roof. But he remains unflaggingly cheerful, Veronica observes, and when the house is finished he lifts up his children in his arms and looks so proud it makes her smile.

That evening, as she sits by the cooking fire, he comes over.

"So, Veronica, it's you next," Wilbur says. He speaks in Juba Arabic; the familiar dialect always makes her feel comfortable.

"Next for what?" asks Veronica, looking up in the semi-darkness.

He crouches down beside her. "You need a proper house! If you are all going to survive the rains you will need a house. You don't think I can sleep safe and dry if my neighbour is sleeping under the sky?"

"I can't afford a house," says Veronica simply, staring at the fire. "We'll be alright in the tent."

"You will not!" retorts Wilbur. "Do you want to be the only one in the settlement without a roof? I have talked to the others," he says, gesturing around at the clutch of half-built houses and makeshift shelters around them. "We are all neighbours now, and we must act like neighbours. We want to help you."

CHAPTER 19

Lilian

January 2017

On food distribution day, Lilian gets up earlier than usual, in the pre-dawn, even before the first of the cockerels have started crowing. She needs to get her chores done early, for today she will stand in line from early morning until the heat of midday, edging forward along roped-off queues under the watch of the World Vision aid workers who are in charge of handing out food in her section of the camp. When she reaches the front she will show her ration card to the official, have her name crossed off his list and crouch down to dip her index finger into purple indelible ink that won't fade for a week. It is a carefully choreographed routine, designed to ensure that refugees cannot cheat the system and claim for food more than once. As a single woman with no dependants, Lilian will receive twelve kilos of maize, nearly three kilos of beans, cooking oil and salt to last her for the whole month. The previous month it was barely enough, and Lilian has become accustomed to a persistent, empty hunger.

Tonight she will eat again, but not too much, because this month she has plans. She is going to sell some of the food and buy herself a new dress. Lilian loves clothes, patterns and fabrics. More than anything, she loves colour and cannot go another day wearing her mother's awful, mud-coloured dress. She has known hunger before, and she is not afraid of it.

She scrutinises the second-hand clothes on sale, arranged in piles on a plastic sheet and categorised by worth. At one end is a useless heap of mismatched, ruined shoes; their display revealing such foolish opportunism on the part of the seller that Lilian nearly marches off without examining the rest. But she perseveres, moving slowly up the line, pausing at the soft pink and yellow baby blankets embroidered with teddy bears that look almost new, and the piles of shorts and T-shirts that would be the right size for Harmony. There is a little stretchy belt, with a silver snake for a clasp. She feels the familiar stabbing pain, just behind her ribs. She digs her fingernails into her palms.

"Boy or girl?" asks the vendor, a solid woman squatting comfortably on her haunches.

Lilian jumps. In her mind she has been dressing her sweet, loving son in his new clothes, seeing him smile.

"No," says Lilian. "No, no." She shakes her head and steps back from the piles of children's clothes. "It's for me. I mean, I'm looking for something for me."

The woman gestures towards the stack at the end. Lilian

crouches down and starts to rummage. There is a black pencil skirt with threads hanging from the hem. Another skirt, dark green, long and pleated. A silky blouse with a bow at the front. A maroon-red top with sequins on the shoulders. Some ordinary T-shirts, their colours faded by washing. A maternity dress in thin denim that would drown her tiny frame. Lilian sighs.

"Take three for ten thousand," the woman says. Lilian straightens up, ready to leave.

"Wait," says the seller, hauling round a big plastic bag from behind her stool. "Then have a look in here. It's all very nice."

Lilian squats down and starts sorting through the bag, handing unwanted garments to the woman as she digs down further. She rejects a blue polka dot dress, a leopard-print skirt, more shabby T-shirts. Then she sees it. A yellow cotton dress with pretty scalloped sleeves and a little tie belt. She stands up, holding it against her. It isn't at all practical for this place, for the sun and the dust.

The woman hones in on the sale.

"Six thousand," she ventures. "It's my best dress. Give me your ration card and pay the other half next month."

"Ha!" Lilian looks up in shock. "Swindler!" she almost spits. What do you take me for?"

She pulls three thousand shillings from the left side of her bra. She has hidden the same amount on the other side. She can feel the ragged notes scratching her skin.

"This is all I have," she says, showing the seller the crumpled, dirty notes.

"What, so I am a fool?" the woman retorts, waving Lilian's hand away in disgust. "Do you want me to starve?"

Lilian tuts, lifting her chin defiantly, stuffing the money back into her bra and letting the dress drop to the woman's lap.

"Forget it," she says, turning to leave. "I can see you are not a serious person."

She has taken only a few steps when the woman calls her back. After a little more haggling, Lilian pulls one more note from the right side of her bra and the two seal the deal quite amicably. The woman folds up the dress and puts it in a thin blue plastic bag.

"It's a good choice," she says, handing it over. "You will look very fine."

CHAPTER 20

January 2017

Bidi Bidi has grown within months to become the biggest refugee camp in the world – and holds that status for a few more months until another refugee crisis explodes half a world away. Everyone outside the settlement says it is a success: refugees live with neighbours from places they have never heard of, from ethnic groups on opposing sides of age-old rivalries, speaking languages they don't recognise. Living in the camp has brought them together. But that doesn't mean everything is forgotten. The refugees are resilient – everyone says that too – but that doesn't mean they are inured to the human suffering and violence they have witnessed.

Rates of sexual violence were epic in South Sudan's war. In a survey carried out at the UN camp in Juba, 70 per cent of the women had been raped, and even more had been forced to witness a sexual assault. Men had been forcibly recruited to armed groups, tortured, clubbed with rifle butts and even raped themselves. Children had seen their siblings slaughtered with machetes or had been separated from their parents in the chaos of a shoot-out. Mothers like Lilian had lost sons or daughters while racing from massacres. In the camp, in the present, there is kindness, but in the realms of memory there is trauma, cruelty and pain.

Officially it is called psycho-social support. Most people call it counselling. There is one specialised mental health agency in the camp, working miracles in a place of overwhelming need. Each week they scrape together the cash needed to buy fuel for the motorcycles and one aged Pajero that their three clinical psychologists and half a dozen counsellors use to get around the vast area of the camp. They go zone by zone, offering mental-health screenings to those who think they might need help. Their questionnaire asks the residents about their feelings, their behaviours and their symptoms – vetting them for anxiety, post-traumatic stress disorder and depression. Are they short-tempered or aggressive? Do they have bad dreams, body aches, loss of appetite? Do they cry all the time? Are they interested in the things that used to give them pleasure? Have they harmed themselves, contemplated suicide? Those identified as needing help are put into groups of twelve and invited to join a programme of counselling.

On Tuesday afternoon the ten women and two men of the newly formed group in Zone One emerge from their shelters and descend the rocky slopes to the meeting place near the dried-up stream. Through the shimmering haze, James bumps into view on his motorbike, heroic in his sunglasses and maroon bomber jacket, dust billowing around him. James is their counsellor. He is always true to his word. If he has promised to find a solution to someone's problem he will do so; if he is unable to help, he will say so too. He is straightforward and always perfectly clear – attributes that are highly valued in the settlement, where the residents crave predictability.

James pulls up, cuts the engine, dismounts and removes his helmet. His smile of greeting reveals a chipped front tooth.

"Ahh, Dorothy! Beatrice! Veronica! Lilian! Jane! How are you?"

How he remembers their names they do not know. His voice is smooth and leisurely; his charm irresistible. Dorothy, a tall, gazelle-like woman in a smart blue jacket, stifles a giggle. Jane, elderly and weathered by worry, dips her head as if to hide a blush. Even Lilian finds she can't help smiling when James is around.

"And Asha!" James waves in greeting towards Lilian's friend who is hurrying towards them, one hand on her belly. She has shut up her liquor stall and has sent the drinkers home early.

"Don't rush!" James calls to her. "Don't rush! We have plenty of time!"

James turns to the others who are squinting beneath the blinding sun. Daniel is there, with Bosco, who is about the same age. They are the only two men in the group. Ideally, James would like to treat the men and women separately, but men are a minority in the camp and more reluctant to come forward for help, so those selected by screening are lumped in with the women.

Daniel and Bosco shield their eyes against the sun, giving James the impression they are saluting him. He greets them with rapid, three-stage handshakes —thumb-over-thumb, thumb-under thumb, thumb-over-thumb. The guys are smiling and expectant.

James pulls out a plastic folder from his satchel. They walk over to the wood-and-tarp community tent where they hold the counselling sessions. *No Health Without Mental Health!* reads a sign next to the flap door. James pulls it back and ushers his clients into the stifling heat.

"Let's get everyone settled, and we can start," he says.

The refugees have been enrolled on a ten-week cognitive behavioural therapy programme especially designed for victims of trauma. They start with controlled breathing to help them relax. *Deep breaths in through the nose, fill your lungs and let your belly swell. Then slowly out through the mouth, one, two, three, that's it.* The first two sessions are called psycho-education. Why do you feel sad or stressed? Why are you aggressive? Why don't you sleep? Why do you keep yourself alone? Why don't you eat? *It is because of your past experiences.* James repeats this over and over, this link between what happened to them during the war in South Sudan to what they are feeling now. The night terrors, the body pains – some of them believe they have been infected with evil. Surely the spirits of the dead are coming back to haunt them?

"It's my son," says Dorothy. "They butchered him. He is not at peace. He is trying to tell me."

"No," says James, firmly. "It is not your son. He is not the one. What you have seen has affected your mind, what happened to your son is affecting your mind. It is all the bad things that happened to you that are causing your symptoms. It is not your son."

James encourages them to do the breathing again and Beatrice talks about what she lost when she fled from South Sudan with her four daughters.

"First we met the rebels; they took my money. Later we were stopped by the Dinka and they stole the rest," she says. "When we got to the settlement I was having a lot of thoughts. My kids would ask for something to eat. I told them I had nothing to give them. I would not eat, not sleep, I kept thinking about how those soldiers had robbed me."

James can empathise. As a child, he lived through a savage civil war in northern Uganda.

"When I was fourteen I missed a year of school," he tells the group. "A whole year! There was no money. My parents planted rice and saved six sacks so I could go back to school. Every day I would sit and look at those sacks, waiting for the term to begin. But one night the rebels came and burned our house and every house along the roadside. My six bags of rice were gone. My school fees were gone."

He sits down to join his clients on the floor, hugging his knees and rocking.

"It hurt me. It really hurt me," he says, rolling the *r* for emphasis. "I was so ashamed to be poor. Life was miserable. But now I have learned something: my bad experiences will only have an effect on my present life if I let them. This is what we all need to learn."

Over the following weeks, in sessions three and four – "behaviour activation" – James helps them explore the link between their feelings and their behaviour. How has your behaviour changed since you got to the settlement? They draw up a list. *These days I don't go out. I stay in my house unless I have to do something like fetch water. I lash out at my family. I quarrel with my neighbour. I used to like to dance and sing. Now I don't do that. I used to cook good food. Now I boil beans.* So, what can they change? They all get homework to complete: Go to church and sing a hymn. Enrol yourself in school. Find a job as a volunteer. Go to fetch firewood by yourself. Start a football team. Chat with your neighbour. Prepare the best meal you can.

By weeks five and six they have progressed to "cognitive coping" – *turn negative thoughts into positive ones, find solutions!*

"You like to think about the okra you used to eat in South Sudan? Yes?" James paces around the circle. "What else, the tomatoes, the onions? Yes? Yes? You miss it, right? You miss it all!"

The group nods in recognition, some clap their hands instinctively; they love to think about the good memories of home. "Well, don't think about it!" James cries, clicking his fingers and bringing them sharply back to the present. "Dig a trench and plant a garden! If you want those things, then help yourself!"

They laugh. Not so easy to grow anything here in this dry, rocky landscape. How would they get seeds before the rains start? But they are excited, not offended. James's positivity, however preposterous, is infectious. He is zealous in his belief in the power of therapy and positive thinking. By the end of each session, the tent is buzzing with ideas and plans.

"Trauma is a wound. If you have a wound and you simply tie it tightly with a piece of cloth and try to forget about it, what will happen?"

Week seven and the group has gathered back in the tent, sitting in a circle on the plastic mat.

Daniel raises his hand. He senses his eagerness is annoying to the others, but he can't help it.

"Yes?"

"It will rot. If you don't clean the wound, if you don't give it air, if you don't change the dressings, it could become infected."

"Exactly!" James responds. "So, what should we do?"

He waits. He would prefer one of the others to answer.

"Yes, Veronica?" Her hand is raised.

Veronica's legs are stretched out in front of her and Sunday is sitting on her lap. Her voice is soft but she speaks slowly and clearly. "We should let the wound breathe. We should look after it until it has healed."

"That's right!" says James, pleased with the youngest member of the group. "Trauma is a wound in a person's life. And the wound is in the brain and is very, very painful. We try to hide it, not talk about it. We don't even want to think about it. We don't want to go back to the wound and feel the pain. But you leave it and the wound rots. No fresh air to dry it. We should untie the wound and wash it and let it breathe. That will be very painful, for a while, but then the wound will start to heal."

Twelve pairs of eyes look at him intently. James knows more about them now. He knows who has been raped, widowed or has lost a child. He knows the woman who is being beaten by her husband. He knows the one who fled from the army after his brother was executed for stealing a rifle. He knows which ones cannot sleep, have unexplained aches and pains or nervous ticks.

"The wound you have in your brain shows itself in fear, in avoiding things, in flashbacks that you can't control," James explains. "You think there is nothing you can do about it? There is. It is called exposure therapy. Exposure therapy," he repeats, drawing out the words, giving time for the translator Lucy to think of the correct terminology in Juba Arabic. "What I want you to do is to tell us what has happened to you, just like it is happening to you now."

"Remember, the ground rules."

It is week eight and the second session of exposure therapy.

"We are all assured of confidentiality," James says. "We do not tell anyone, our husbands, our wives, our children, our chickens . . . no one. Does everyone understand?"

The group murmurs its agreement.

"And when we tell our stories we always tell it like it is happening to us, right now." He holds his hands near his lips in a prayer position. "Don't be afraid. Don't hold back. We care about you. If you need to cry, you cry. Do not feel judged. We are here to help each other. We are here to understand our memories."

Around the circle they tell their stories. Some of the women hold hands. Dorothy is watching as rebel fighters tie up her son with his own clothes and cut him to pieces. They say he is a traitor. She is running away. She is still wearing the same blue jacket she was wearing on that day.

Mary sees the government soldiers at her door; they burst in, they ransack her house, they steal her money, she had almost a hundred dollars saved. Three of her neighbours are killed putting up a fight. "Right, now, we must run!" Mary cries out. She's talking to her husband. He refuses to leave, he is rooted to the spot. His eyes are wide open but his body is frozen; he doesn't respond to her pleas. She is running, carrying her child on her pregnant belly. She doesn't know where she is going.

Asha is next. She lives in Juba with her husband and son. They have three rooms with a cement floor and a corrugated metal roof. They have curtains and a mattress, a full cooking set. She eats meat twice a week. Everyone sighs – life in South Sudan doesn't get much better, but they know it's about to take a turn for the worse. She's at work at the nursery school. They are putting the children down for their afternoon naps, including her own son, when the shooting starts. *Boom! Boom! Boom!* She needs to get home; she runs through the streets with her son; he's stumbling, they are in the road, she sees a sniper, they are about to die. She picks up her child, he is six and he is heavy, she puts him on her back like a sack of rice and she runs, through the bullets, all the way to her house.

They speak succinctly, matter-of-factly. Some members of the group wipe away tears. The memories hurt. There is silence. Mary raises her hand, she wants to add something. Of course, James says, please continue. Mary wasn't going to tell them this, she hadn't felt it was right, but now the others had spoken so openly, she thinks she should tell them. Continue, says James, say whatever you want.

"I'm on my way," says Mary. "I'm footing. I am trying to carry my child but sometimes she must walk. We are together with some neighbours in a group. There are soldiers on the road. They are wearing uniform. One grabs me, in front of the others. I scream to them to hold my child. To cover her eyes. One soldier has his way with me," says Mary, looking around the group, emboldened, unashamed, her baby latched onto her breast, his eyelids half closed in satisfaction. "Afterwards I just think, I'm glad I am pregnant already. At least he couldn't do that to me." Mary shifts her baby to the other breast and tucks her exposed nipple back into her bra. She turns to her neighbour.

It's Veronica. "Would you like to speak?" James asks. She has been wondering what to say, whether to tell the others everything or nothing at all. They all seem much older, she is just a child. There are men here too. What would they think? But everyone's honesty has inspired her. The boy Daniel told them about how he escaped from Juba, on the same night she escaped with Jackson to the UN base. Then he told them about the car crash and how he had let his father down. He was a Dinka, Veronica should hate him, but she finds she doesn't. Bosco's story is also sad. And last week Lilian told them how she had lost her son. He must be dead, Veronica thought at the time, but she didn't say so.

When it comes to her turn she finds it easy. She tells them

about how her mother abandoned her that night, how her two brothers are missing and how she had to get Sunday and her little sister to the border with no money. She sees the scene so clearly in her head. The soldier is stopping her, the woman she is with says something to him. The soldier, whose hand is bleeding, raises his rifle and shoots the woman in the chest. For no reason. She slumps to the ground and blood spreads around her. Her mouth is open. No one goes to help her. Veronica can't move. The children are wailing. Veronica is shaking. The soldier is calm. He asks them if they need a ride to the border. He has a pickup. Veronica says she has no choice. She has to go with him. She climbs in the cab. She sits nearest the soldier and leans over to pull in Amani and Sunday. She must protect them from this man. Blood is seeping from his hand. Sweat is dripping down his face to the collar of his camouflage jacket. He stinks. He can do anything to us, Veronica is thinking. He will defile us at least. He will probably kill us. She tries to smile at him but she can't stop her body shaking. They drive along the rutted highway. They are waved through checkpoints, this man seems important. They crawl to a halt. There are buses, trucks, cars. People everywhere.

"This is the border," the soldier says. "Uganda." With a flick of his head he signals they should get out. He's just dropping them off, they are free to go. It's as if he's a taxi driver and we are his customers, Veronica tells the group. To this day, she doesn't understand why he did it.

She finishes talking, and realises she is tearful. She wipes her nose on the back of her hand. Sunday is standing now, by her head, so close she can hear her daughter's soft breathing.

CHAPTER 21

Lilian

February 2017

Lilian's neighbour Asha is her best friend in the camp. They are different sorts of people – Asha is quiet and serious-minded – but they are a similar age and get on well. Her son Dumo is seven, a year older than Harmony. Asha is always sensitive when she talks about him to Lilian. She tries hard to imagine how Lilian might feel and Lilian appreciates her kindness.

Asha started a home-brew business to buy some shoes for Dumo. After one of his green plastic sandals broke beyond repair he limped off to school with just one shoe. After a week or so that shoe went missing. Dumo didn't say anything about it, but his friend told Asha that someone had shouted bad names at Dumo and had grabbed it and run off with it in the play yard. Dumo didn't run after him or even tell the teacher, the boy said. He just went over to the metal-framed swing set that no one used in the heat of the day and sat on its hot rubber seat and waited for the bell to signal the start of afternoon lessons.

He never complains to his mother, but Asha has noticed his increasing reluctance to go to school. When he leaves in the morning he seems to walk impossibly slowly up the rise to the main track. Just one word from her and he'd turn back to the house to stay at home. But she doesn't say anything. His education is the most important thing in their lives. His school is a concrete shell; there are 120 children in his class with an eight-year age range from youngest to eldest. Some have to stand. It is hardly the schooling she wants for him, but it is still an education. She wants to save up and buy him new sandals so he can go to school with pride.

The first customers of the day are always Charles and Michael. The two are good-natured drunks, happy to numb their days away under the tree next to the wooden washing-up stand that Asha has built for herself. Charles and Michael generate a minuscule but consistent income by selling part of their food rations each month. Their smiles are broad, but their eyes are bloodshot and their skin has a jaundiced tinge. Her best customers will not live long, Asha always says.

Lilian despises the drunks – Charles, Michael, all of them. Back in South Sudan, she and Samuel never drank a drop of alcohol, they couldn't afford to waste their lives like that. She never really complains – she understands why Asha needs the business – but she hates it when the drinkers lope into their little shady enclosure and plonk themselves on the little wooden stools under the tree. They are lazy, work-shy, undeserving layabouts, she thinks. The refugee life suits them. They have failed; failed their parents, their wives and their children and now all they want to do is drink themselves into an early grave. Lilian has no time for such men, but now she has her volunteering job she is away from the house most days anyway. She's helping others again, not in the same warm-hearted, compassionate way in which she went about life when Samuel and Harmony were with her, but with a detached, practical manner more suited to her new circumstances. It gives her a sense of satisfaction, and keeps her busy all of her waking hours. She gets home at about five o'clock, leaving just an hour or so of daylight left to get the fire going.

One day, Lilian has finished work and is walking back to her hut. Asha, Charles and Michael are standing there, looking up the slope towards her. They seem to be waiting for her. The men look strangely sober for so late in the day, agitated even, shuffling from foot to foot. Asha stands straight, her eyes wide, her body still as if she is holding her breath. Lilian frowns. An image of Harmony pops into her head. She banishes it.

"What is it?" she asks as she comes closer. "Why are you waiting for me? What is it?"

"There is a boy . . ." Asha begins. "Well, we've heard there is a boy."

Lilian stops dead still. She stares. She swallows.

"We haven't met him," says Michael, "He's in Zone Three, the boy. He's six, I think."

Lilian doesn't speak.

"One of the other men told us about him," Michael goes on. "He came by himself, the boy, to the settlement. He lives with a woman, but she is not his mother."

Charles takes over. "She's sick. She can't look after him. She wants to find his mother. He's about seven, I think . . . he's a good boy, by all accounts. But he is a mouth to feed." He laughs weakly.

"He came in August last year, or September," says Michael.

"Could have been July," Charles ventures. "She found him alone, he was footing it to Uganda, without anyone. He's in Zone Three, he's living with—"

Lilian holds up two hands, and steps back, poised, as if she's about to sprint away. She closes her eyes. She breathes in through her nose. "Please," she says very quietly, exhaling. She pushes air down with her hands, trying to slow them down. "Please," she says. "Who has told you this?"

The story continues in a rapid jumble of inexact explanations, worrying contradictions and generous gesticulations. Charles and Michael are enjoying the novelty of having something useful to say. Asha coaxes them along; she understands so well the significance of what it could mean. Lilian has to interrupt, repeatedly, seeking clarifications, detail.

Earlier in the day, a man had come from Zone Three. He was a customer, a drinker. Asha's brew has gained a reputation in the camp; it is pure and cheap and worth the walk. Once she served him, Asha didn't stay around, she needed to split some firewood and she left them to it, she tells Lilian, apologetically. How she wishes she'd been there. The man got talking, he talked about lots of things; Charles and Michael were only half listening. Then he mentioned the boy, how the subject had come up they couldn't really recall. The man had a neighbour, a woman. That woman, when she had been running from South Sudan, had found a boy on the way – he was alone and had lost his parents. She'd brought him with her, she'd even carried him some of the way when he was too weak and tired. That's what the man said. The boy was six or seven, he was no trouble but the woman wondered if his parents were still alive somewhere. That was all. The man talked about other things then, about the truck he used to own, the places he had been. But he didn't say any more about the boy.

"But where is he now, the man, where is he?" asks Lilian urgently.

"He's gone," says Charles. "He drank up and left. It was only after he'd gone that we thought about you. And your son. We thought, 'Maybe the boy is Lilian's boy?' So we've been standing here waiting, waiting for you to come back."

Lilian lies awake all night, turning over the possibilities in her head. There are many children in the camp, maybe thousands, who have been separated from their parents. Harmony is not the only missing child. There are so many young boys like him looking for their mothers. But there is something about how they described this boy that gives her hope. He was a good boy, well behaved. Hadn't she brought Harmony up to be respectful? He was young, but he knew his manners. Yet really, that could be any boy. She knows she shouldn't get carried away. She can't even try to sleep.

She gets up, crouches in the doorway of her home and looks up at the nearly full moon. Is Harmony lying under the same moon? She stays there, rocking slowly back and forth, waiting for the morning.

CHAPTER 22

Daniel

March 2017

They play the match in the golden hour as the sun dips down towards the low hills. Even then there is no escape from the exhausting heat; it rises up thickly from the baked earth, wrapping itself around the spectators who have lined the pitch, their arms draped over one another's shoulders. On one side, under a wide, leafy tree, are the villagers, men in knitted caps – the older ones sitting on wooden stools – young boys in football shirts and girls with white headscarves tied at the back. On the other are the refugees, a shabbier crowd made up mostly of men. A shimmering haze sits over the pitch, all dry dust and sticks of yellow grass; Daniel inspected it when he took the team out to warm up. He put the boys in a circle and took them through their exercises – hamstring stretches, hip sways, high knees and heel kicks, skipping, side gallops and jumping jacks. The other team has a black-and-white striped kit, matching socks and proper football boots. Daniel has managed to get his hands on a full set of fluorescent green tabards for his side; their footwear is a mishmash of old trainers and borrowed boots with studs. Focus on yourselves, on your game, he tells the boys. Stay in your positions and let the other team worry about themselves.

The under-seventeen team was only formed a few weeks ago and this is their first match outside the settlement. They are playing a side from the village of Bilijia, a simple, well-swept hamlet just off the bumpy road to Yumbe. Now that most people in the camp have built their own houses, it is not always clear where the settlement ends and the host community – as it is known – begins. The main differences are that the Ugandans whitewash their houses to halfway up the walls, they have more animals, better soil and enjoy the shade of the mighty mango trees. This one is a Muslim village, but others are Christian. The boys on the other team are bigger and better fed than his, Daniel notices; their goalkeeper looks like a fully grown man.

The teams run on to the pitch to a roar from the crowd. Men with sticks patrol the perimeter, keeping toes behind the touchlines. It is a powerful, physical game. Daniel loves hearing the dull thud of the ball, the shouts and swearing and the close-up drama. He yells encouragement as one of his star boys dispossesses an opposition forward and tears up the wing.

"Man on!" Daniel yells. "Pass it!"

Too late, the black-and-white stripes are back on the ball and advancing out of their half in fluid formation. Glancing up briefly, the midfielder floats a long ball into the box, and their striker sprints to get his boot to it.

"Offside!" Daniel screams. The referee is slow on his feet, out of position. The striker slams the ball just beyond the right-hand goal post and it flies hard into the crowd.

"Focus!" Daniel bellows, forming a megaphone with his hands. "Concentrate!" He feels light-headed. He hasn't eaten. He is still on the host's side of the pitch, standing in a small exclusion zone that the villagers have vacated around him. "Get back in position!"

They don't seem to be listening. The refugees' goalkeeper kicks the ball back up the pitch, but of the two players who jump to control it, it is the taller opposition boy who wins. A swift break, some quick passes and bang, this time the shot is on target. Daniel's goalkeeper dives in vain to the rock-hard ground. The crowd around Daniel cheer and clap, pushing forward for a view of the striker's celebrations and filling the space around him. Daniel doesn't have a watch but it feels like less than five minutes in and they are already a goal down.

By half-time the players are gasping for breath and gleaming with sweat. The village women carry gourds of water on to the pitch and the boys pour it into their mouths and over their heads. They pant through Daniel's pep talk, bent over with their hands on their knees. They have conceded a further two goals.

"This is your match to take," Daniel tells them calmly; his even voice disguising the frustration and downright competitiveness he feels inside. "Just think where you have come from! What you have done! You are all strong boys," he says, channelling his counsellor, James. "You are small, yes, you are poor, yes, but you can beat this team!"

The boys' heads are down. They can hear the home crowd on the mango-tree side, talking and laughing and sensing victory.

"Look up!" Daniel commands. Eleven pairs of eyes meet his, disconsolate. Daniel straightens up to his full height, towering over all of them. A line of sweat slithers down his forehead. "You have the courage to win," he says, warming to his theme. "Today you are representing all of us! Everyone in the settlement! Everyone in South Sudan! Go out there and win!"

Football is probably the one consistently positive thing in Daniel's life. Miraculously, his legs have healed, he only feels them ache when it is cool and cloudy. But he can't play football anymore, and he misses it. He misses the freedom he used to feel running up the wing. He misses using the ball skills he had practised for hours and hours, first in the camp in Kenya, then back in South Sudan, then at school in Uganda. He misses the thrill of scoring a goal. In 2010 he had been picked from hundreds of boys in the Kakuma refugee camp to go to Dodoma in Tanzania for a football tournament. To his mother's amazement, the organisers chartered a plane for the team and they all flew for the first time in their lives, down over Kenya's Rift Valley and past the snow-capped Mount Kilimanjaro. In Juba, after his accident, he had become a coach and it had been going well, until the war cut things short, again. In the camps, at school, everywhere he had been, the common denominator has been football. It doesn't matter who is Ugandan or Sudanese,

Dinka or Nuer, football unites them, it is something they all understand. In northern Uganda, where he went to school, everyone supports Arsenal; a Fly Emirates shirt is a young man's uniform. Some of the South Sudanese, though, favour Manchester United. Having been told at an early age that his absent father was also a fan, Daniel is devoted to them too.

When James encouraged him to think of something positive to do, football was the obvious first step. Once he decided to do it, he felt energised in a way he hadn't felt in months. He went around all the after-school clubs in Zones One and Two – peace clubs they were called – where adolescents were allowed to hang out after school. Their purpose was to promote good relations between young people whose families might be fighting each other back in South Sudan. The clubs were run by aid agencies that held talks about post-conflict reconciliation, sex, contraception and domestic violence, as well as organising talent competitions, poetry reading and games. Daniel managed to borrow a marker pen and big piece of pink card from one of the peace club leaders to make signs to say he was looking for young football talent in order to form a team. He pinned them up at the schools, at the after-school clubs and the clinic. Then he booked the playground of the zone's kindergarten to use for trials and training and set about procuring some kit.

The whistle blows for the second half and the spirited home crowd starts up a haphazard Mexican wave behind their goalkeeper that ripples up their side of the pitch with cheers and raised arms. Daniel is the only one who fails to comply.

His brow is knitted in concentration, his arms are crossed defensively over his chest; he looks the part of a professional football manager looking on in helpless agony. Ten minutes in and the village team scores again, this time from a free kick lobbed gracefully over their opponent's hesitant defensive wall. The village drummers start up right behind Daniel; the women next to him clap and sway as the quickening beats rise to a crescendo.

"Mark your men!" Daniel yells uselessly into the din. "Keep calm! Keep passing!"

Dusk is descending and his boys look tired. One is limping with cramp. Daniel hasn't brought substitutes. He sees that some of the men who have walked from the camp to watch the match have squatted down on their haunches, exhausted by the tension of losing. They haven't the money to buy the fruit-flavoured drinks or the little bags of popcorn on sale. Suddenly, his young star Emmanuel is racing up the wing on the far side with a fresh burst of energy, bypassing one opponent and wrong-footing another. He dribbles to the edge of the penalty box. Daniel notices the goalkeeper is off his line.

"Just shoot!" he screams.

A defender launches himself at Emmanuel with two feet, bringing them both down yards from the goal. The referee, racing up the pitch, blows his whistle and points at the ground.

"Penalty!" Daniel is jumping up and down. The spectators around him are exclaiming with fake outrage; Daniel ignores them. "Penalty!" he yells again.

It is happening. The referee is waving away the players

around him who have launched a half-hearted protest. Emmanuel has picked himself up and has seized the ball from a spectator behind the goal. He carefully places it down where the referee indicates the penalty spot should be and takes five measured steps back. The goalkeeper jogs up and down, flapping his arms.

Daniel murmurs a prayer. Just one goal, please God, just one goal. As Emmanuel launches towards the ball, Daniel looks down at his feet. The people around him let out a disappointed moan and Daniel raises his head to see the travelling fans on the far side jumping around and clutching each other with joy.

Daniel bites into his smile. He slaps his fist into his palm. For a first match, it is a respectable result.

CHAPTER 23

Veronica

March 2017

Under the oversight of Bidi Bidi's commander, an authoritative man quick to make decisions and assign duties, responsibility for certain functions in each area of the camp has been divided up among the aid agencies. For example, in Zone Five, Plan International is in charge of education and World Vision is responsible for child protection. In Zone Three, the International Rescue Committee takes the lead on construction and health. Although it has never been explained to him, Veronica's neighbour Wilbur has a good grasp of the system. He made enquiries and believes that Save the Children is responsible for construction in Zone One, where they live. The budget doesn't stretch to handing out construction materials and tools to everyone and most refugees have to fend for themselves. But the most vulnerable, including the elderly, disabled and sick are prioritised. They are allocated a permanent house with a brick-built latrine nearby that they share with the surrounding community.

Veronica's family has not yet appeared on any priority list, perhaps surprisingly given hers is a so-called child-headed household. But in a place of such tremendous need, Veronica seems competent and in control; she hasn't asked for help, so the camp's aid workers have been happy for her to get on with it. But Wilbur sees her vulnerability. It is not just for comfort that Veronica and the two girls need a proper home; it is for survival. Three months of rain under a flimsy, leaking plastic sheet could very well kill them. Pneumonia, diarrhoea, malaria – the children would be prey to them all. Then there are the dangers of the wild – snakes, scorpions and rats – as well as the risk that human predators pose to three undefended girls. After Christmas, Wilbur's wife quietly pointed out the swell in Veronica's belly. The family needs a home, and Wilbur is determined to help them get it.

One Monday morning, Wilbur and Veronica are on the back of a *boda-boda* on the bumpy road to Yumbe, the trading town outside the camp that has boomed with the influx of aid agencies assisting in the refugee operation. Wilbur sits behind the driver and Veronica is squashed behind him, precariously balanced side-saddle. The bike whips up grit from the road that settles in a mask on Veronica's face. It's the first time since she arrived nine months ago that she's left the settlement. They ride past well-stocked shops along the main street selling plastic goods, electronics, bottled beer, boxes of biscuits, and bright clothes displayed on hangers. It's just after nine in the morning, and soft-rock ballads are already blaring from a bar on the corner. They take a left turn past a petrol station and the low-slung bike bounces down a rutted track to a gate with a red Save the Children sign. Wilbur and Veronica dismount and brush themselves down.

A guard pokes his head through the small metal door. "Who are you here to see?"

"I'm not sure," Wilbur says. "I have brought my neighbour, from the settlement. She's in a bad situation. She needs housing. She's still sleeping outside."

Veronica's head is down, her eyes smarting from the dust.

The guard ushers them into the walled compound and points to the visitors' book on a trestle table in front of his sentry box. Wilbur picks up a biro, anchored to the table by a piece of string. He writes down their names. The guard looks at the entry suspiciously, picks up the book and takes it to the solid bungalow that serves as the Save the Children office. He returns to his post without another word.

The visitors are left standing in the shade of the wall. Three minibuses are parked up and their drivers are sitting under a lean-to at the side of the building smoking and drinking coffee. Crates of bottled soda are stacked up by the door. Five staff members with bright red Save the Children vests come out and pile into one of the vehicles; as their driver reverses from the parking space the guard jumps up to open the gate for them. A few minutes later and another group arrives. They greet the guard, smile at Veronica and Wilbur, and walk straight into the office. An hour goes by. It's getting hot. The guard ignores them. There is laughter and chatter coming from the lean-to. The radio is on. A red T-shirted man has joined the drivers, sipping coffee from a plastic mug. He looks across and spots Wilbur and Veronica sheltering in a diminishing sliver of shade. He strides over, mug in hand.

"Good morning," he smiles. "I'm Sadiq." He holds out his hand for the visitors to shake. Sadiq is tall and broad, with a smooth, deep voice and a full beard. "Is someone helping you?"

Veronica can count on her fingers the few people who have helped her in her life. Wilbur, and now Sadiq, will become among the most important. There are a few elements of luck: Sadiq is a child-protection officer who happens to work in her zone in the settlement. He is also kind. He invites the visitors into the office, offers them tea, coffee or soda, and enquires whether they need to use the bathroom. They decline politely. Sadiq pulls up two chairs to his desk and they all sit down. Wilbur is smiling; he looks relieved, thinks Veronica. Despite his good intentions, she knows he could not have taken on her problems as well as his own.

Sadiq takes down Veronica's details: where she is from, where she lives, what school level she has reached. He notes down the names and ages of her dependants – her younger sister, her daughter . . . Veronica breaks off. She looks to Wilbur. He nods his reassurance.

"And . . . well . . . I am expecting," she says, her eyes quickly scanning the open-plan office to see if anyone is listening.

"I see," says Sadiq, looking up. "How many months?"

"I'm not sure. Soon. It's coming soon. I went to the clinic but they didn't tell me much." Her chair scrapes on the floor as she pulls it closer to Sadiq's desk. "I was dizzy, I thought I had malaria, but then we discovered it was . . . this." Veronica looks down at the curve of her belly.

Sadiq frowns. He writes it all down.

"Don't worry," he says. His voice is calm. "We're going to help you."

A week has passed and Veronica wakes up before the children. It's barely light but already warm. For the past few days the camp has been gripped by an extreme heat that rises to a searing crescendo by the middle of the day. The atmosphere is taut and electric, even the birds have been silenced. It feels like everyone is holding their breath. Something has to give; it will start raining soon. Veronica kneels next to their listing shelter and prays, giving thanks for everything she can think of. Then she breaks up some twigs from the top of the woodpile, makes a perfect pyramid of kindling and relights the embers of the fire. Yesterday she sold some of her food rations to buy tea leaves and sugar and she's going to brew it up and offer it to everyone who comes to help.

Sadiq has organised the delivery of the building materials for a new house. There are two thousand bricks and eighteen grass bundles for the roof. Veronica herself went in search of pieces of suitable timber for the door frame. The refugees have to walk further and further for firewood now as they gradually strip away the land around them. It has taken her two days to find tree branches that are long and straight enough. She has also collected some empty USAID vegetable oil tins, to be hammered flat and nailed together to make a new front door.

When the sun comes up they emerge from their houses: Wilbur and his wife, another couple whose daughter plays with Amani, the boys who live next to the dried-up creek, their mother and their grandmother. Veronica starts to hand out the mugs of tea, and the young men that Wilbur has enlisted from his church arrive too. The air is still soft; they want to start work before it gets too hot.

Wilbur takes charge, consulting with Veronica about the best aspect for her new home and marking out its foundations. Together the volunteers dig a shallow square trench in the scorched ground. The door will face west, like the others. Then the men begin to lay the clay bricks as directed by Wilbur while the women set up a relay to bring water from the standpipe to set them together. They will build to above head-height, with no windows; the house needs to be cool. Veronica tries to help, but she's told to sit and watch from the shade of the tree. Nobody has talked about it, but her pregnancy is now plain to see. They are here to help her, they say. She takes the little ones to the wooden plank bench and watches as more than a dozen people, who just months ago had been strangers, build her new home. The children play together, chasing each other around the tree.

By the time Sadiq arrives, the volunteers have already laid three brick courses. Aid workers and non-residents are only permitted to be in the settlement during office hours and it is already after nine. The menacing sun is creeping higher. Sadiq jumps from his vehicle and walks around the new construction, admiring the workmanship, thanking the helpers. He goes over to Veronica, hands in pockets, his smile wide.

"Soon you will be sleeping in luxury!" he says, planting himself next to her on the narrow bench. "And just in time.

It will be raining soon."

Veronica looks down at her hands and sees that she is trembling. Tears well in her eyes. The kindness of her new community is almost more than she can bear. Sadiq leans back a little to pull out a handkerchief from his jeans pocket and offers it to her. Veronica wipes her eyes and blows her nose noisily. Sadiq smiles. Veronica giggles, sniffs, swallows, dabs her eyes again and hands back the soiled square of cotton. They watch the work continue, brick by brick, as the heat presses down.

"Tell me about what happened . . . how you have ended up here, like this," Sadiq asks gently.

It is a professional question; Sadiq needs to know her full story. Sitting next to him, in the shade, Veronica feels comfortable.

She tells Sadiq about her father, her memories of him, how he died so suddenly and how quickly her world changed. How she wishes she could still be a child in Bentiu – they had nothing there really, but, looking back, she feels she had everything. In some ways she is relieved her father is no longer alive though – she would be so ashamed if he could see what has happened to her. Pregnant again! She is not yet eighteen. She tells Sadiq about Jackson and how their relationship began. She should have been stronger, she says. Jackson was good to her, she misses him, but they were too young, she realises that now. She hasn't seen him since July; he disappeared with Riek's men, just like her mother. She hasn't heard from him. He doesn't even know that she is in Uganda with Sunday. Someone told her that he is probably in Congo now, but she isn't sure. He doesn't have a phone and neither does she.

"And your mother?" asks Sadiq. "Do you know where she is?"

"No," Veronica says, looking straight ahead. "We each went in our own direction. She went with the rebels. That was her choice. I am taking care of the family now."

"Do you want me to try to trace her?" asks Sadiq. "We have done that for a lot of people now. You would be surprised, sometimes we are successful."

Veronica looks at Sadiq for a moment, considering his request. "I don't think so," she says. "If Mummy wants to find us, she will."

The two fall into silence, watching the volunteer builders as they start on a new row of bricks. The sun beats down, there's not a breath of wind. The workers seem to be flagging. Veronica can see sweat glistening on the back of Wilbur's neck. Sunday and the other children have started to squabble over a rope swing that Wilbur has made for them.

"Right," says Sadiq, standing up and clapping his hands. The women in the water chain stop and look up. Wilbur's wife wipes the back of her hand across her forehead.

"Thank you, everyone, thank you!" Sadiq continues, shifting into authoritative mode. "Your work is much appreciated. Look at the progress already! But it's getting hot so you should all take a break. I have sodas and samosas for everyone in the car."

The workers down tools and the children sprint to the Save the Children van, jostling to be first in line as Sadiq hauls open the sliding side door. He has crates of Pepsi, Stoney and Mountain Dew, and a big plastic bucket of samosas. Treats like this are rare in the settlement. Veronica stays where she is on the bench. She does not deserve lunch, or any of this, she thinks. She finds their kindness overwhelming.

A few nights later and a booming clap of thunder finally breaks the tension in the humid, charged air. The wind whips up in gusts and the rain that has held back for months is unleashed onto the thirsty soil in relentless, pounding torrents. Veronica and the two girls are ensconced in their new house, sitting side-by-side on a soft cotton sheet on their foam mattress. The door is bolted shut but the lightning flashes through the gap around the frame, illuminating the scene in split-second animations. The girls are not scared. They are sitting together, smiling, holding hands. They are enjoying the smell of the wet earth, the drama of the thunder and the muffled drum of rain on their watertight roof.

CHAPTER 24

Lilian

March 2017

At first light Lilian ties a scarf around her head and starts out for Zone Three. Reaching the top of the small rise behind her home, she can see Bidi Bidi stretched to the hazy horizon. A messy, unshaded city of thatch and white plastic scars the landscape in every direction. The population rouses, moves into action, collecting water and firewood and lighting fires while it is still dry. A few early risers greet her politely. Children walk in groups to school, exercise books balanced expertly on their heads. Lilian is wearing her worn-out rubber sandals. She has not eaten; she has not had anything to drink. She tries to remember the breathing exercises she learned with James. She keeps walking, her back to the rising sun, just like she did when she left South Sudan. Recently, she has allowed herself to think about Harmony, something she started to do after she finished her last therapy session.

But she only allows those thoughts in controlled, bite-sized chunks. She has gone through her pregnancy and Harmony's birth. She has recalled the precious nights she spent with him in his first few months of life, cocooned together, drifting in and out of sleep. She has thought about the day she bought him his first pair of shoes. She saved so hard for those. Cutting his hair for the first time, feeding him. She keeps walking, stopping occasionally on the disorienting grid of dust tracks to ask directions. It's just after ten o'clock when she reaches the Red Cross tent, emblazoned with its iconic branding, a line of majestic Land Cruisers with big bendy radio aerials lined up outside. The set-up commands respect, even in this desperate, lost corner. She walks purposefully up to the reception desk. Lilian has never been intimidated by officialdom.

"I am looking for my child," she says, clearly, matter-of-factly.

The woman does not look up. She is scratching a pay-as-you-go card to reveal the code that will top up the credit on her phone. She blows the metal shavings across the wooden table towards Lilian. She punches the code into her phone, checks her balance and, satisfied, looks up.

"Please repeat," she says.

"I am looking for my child," Lilian repeats.

The woman sighs. She opens the notebook in front of her and picks up her pen.

"Name, date of birth, place of birth," the woman asks.

Lilian carefully gives the details, making sure the woman's notes, written in laboured capital letters, are correct.

"But he doesn't know his date of birth. My son, I mean. If

you ask him. He knows he is six, but he doesn't know the day he was born, exactly."

The woman is not interested in Lilian's clarification. "Date and place last seen," she continues.

Lilian swallows. She relays the information as images of the flames and terror of Ombachi crackle in her head. She wets her lips and swallows, trying to stay calm.

"What is your relationship to the child?"

"I am his mother." She squeezes her hands together.

"Village and zone?" the woman asks. "Pink card number?"

Lilian obliges.

"Do you have a phone?"

"No."

"Right. We will register your child as missing. If he is traced, we will come to your place and find you."

The woman shuts the notebook and keeps her palm on the cover as if holding it closed. Her eyes wander back to her phone.

"But I think he may be here, right here, in this zone," says Lilian, her voice rising. "I have his photo here," she adds quickly, pulling out the mother-and-son portrait she has tucked inside her dress. "Maybe someone has seen him?"

The woman examines the photo and then looks up, taking in Lilian, with her camp-worn face and grubby dress, for the first time. Then she stares back down at the clean, smiling faces in the photographer's studio and then back up again at Lilian, searching for a resemblance.

"I will check for you," she says, finally. She lets out a long breath as if to express the tedium of the task ahead. "You can find a seat outside."

*

Lilian waits outside the tent all day. There is a row of plastic chairs under an awning but she prefers to pace. It is a busy place, lots of coming and going. Two women carrying babies, another woman with three young children, a single man, an older couple. They all have a story, they have lost someone, they are looking for someone, that's why they are here. She sees a boy who could be Harmony's age, and catches herself manoeuvring round to the doorway so she can see his face.

She has trained herself not to do that, not to check every child in case it is Harmony, but she can't stick to her rules any more. She feels alert, alive. She knows it isn't sensible but she can't dampen her expectations now, it's too late.

She doesn't feel hungry or thirsty, but she realises her mouth is dry because she's having trouble swallowing. She darts round to the toilets and drinks from the drum of water outside that is supposed to be for hand-washing, stooping so she can drink from the plastic tap. The water is warm and gritty. She takes another handful and washes her face, blinking as drips fall on to her dress. She scuttles back to the entrance.

The woman at reception came out at lunchtime and walked down to the market. She is back at her desk now. She sees Lilian, but pretends she hasn't. Lilian wants to go back inside and remind her she is waiting – has there been any news? She marches through the doorway into the stuffy heat of the tent but swings round again in a single move, out into the harsh sunlight. She doesn't want to annoy the woman – there are lots of people she needs to help. She's probably sent someone out already to look for Harmony, Lilian thinks. It's probably best if I just wait here.

By five o'clock the guard is rolling down the tarpaulin flaps to close up the tent, securing the bottom with wooden pegs. The sky is grey and low; it will rain soon. The receptionist leaves with the other Red Cross workers, avoiding eye contact with Lilian, who is the only one left waiting outside. The staff members pile into the cars to be driven back to Yumbe. Lilian stands staring at the tent for a while. The guard has taken a seat for the night on one of the chairs under the narrow shelter of the awning. He seems uncomfortable under Lilian's gaze, but says nothing. Eventually, she turns away and walks in the direction of home, just as the rain starts to fall.

Each morning brings fresh hope. She repeats the exercise for the next three days – rising early, walking miles across the settlement, waiting, returning. She has barely washed or eaten. Asha looks at her friend's raw-bone face, her filthy dress, and wishes she hadn't said anything at all. The drinkers, what did they know? They were losers, drinking themselves to death in a refugee camp. Who could blame them, embellishing their pasts, gilding their stories.

The one about the little boy made them feel important. They saw the reaction in Lilian's face – the panic, the hope – and they knew it was a big deal. Now, every time Lilian comes back alone, silent, past the tree where they sit, swaying with exhaustion, they feel disappointment too. They wanted to be part of her story, part of a miracle, but miracles never happen in Bidi Bidi. Charles clicks his tongue against the top of his mouth and Asha distractedly refills the drinking mugs, her eye on Lilian's closed door.

The Red Cross office is closed on Saturday and Lilian stays inside her hut. She emerges late in the day to wash her dress, ready for church. She hangs it up and retreats back into her house. On Sunday morning she gets up at the usual hour, cooks her breakfast and goes back inside to change. She has braided her hair. She walks to church with Asha and Dumo. The young boy looks at her curiously. Lilian seems to speak as normal but there is something robotic about her. Her face is stiff. She has been coated in a clear, hard shell. She sings the hymns and prays with her usual verve. She crosses herself as she leaves the unadorned hall, bows her head and walks straight home, bolting the door behind her.

Asha sends Dumo off to play and waits outside Lilian's hut. The hours pass, but she remains by the door, like a faithful dog.

The door clunks open.

"I could hear you there," says Lilian, squinting in the bright light of the afternoon. "Sitting there. Breathing. It was disturbing me. Why are you sitting there? You are behind on your work."

She is trying to sound irritated, yet light-hearted. She can't keep up the pretence for long. She stumbles to the bench and crumples down next to Asha. Asha strokes Lilian's braided head as her friend sobs into her lap. She lets her heave out loud, wounded sobs. Asha understands. Lilian howls and sniffs until she has almost fallen asleep, her face lying on Asha's thighs.

"What do you want to do?" Asha asks softly.

There is a long pause.

"I want to go back," Lilian whispers, looking up. "To the Red Cross. I want to keep asking them. I can't stop it."

"It's all right," says Asha. "It's all right. I'm going to come with you."

They get there first thing on Monday just as the watchman is rolling up the tent doors and the big cars are starting to arrive from town. Lilian feels fresh again. She has a new plan and that plan is to come here every day until she has found Harmony. She explained it all to Asha on the way and her friend did not respond in words but she took her hand and squeezed it. The receptionist lady seems unnerved, almost annoyed, to see Lilian again. She has no news, she tells them, and she doesn't recommend waiting. If they get any new information they will come to Zone One and tell her in person.

They wait anyway, on the white plastic chairs outside. Deep down, Lilian knows it isn't sensible but Asha hasn't tried to persuade her out of it. She's grateful for that. It's nice for them to be able to sit in the comfort of the shade without the usual tasks and chores. The neighbours will fetch their water for them today and they will tell the drinkers there will be no service. The small community they have created is strong. They are Madi, Kakwa, Nuer, Kuku and Bari; all from different places, now living like a clan. It hasn't been easy but even in this new land, this new society, they have retained the traditions of supporting each other as neighbours – traditions that have sustained them all through war and struggle.

But they miss the old life too. Running here, on foot, they have lost everything: their homes; their land; their cattle. So many have lost a mother, a son or a husband.

"I wish I knew how happy I was," says Lilian, gazing across the bleak, unyielding expanse of the camp. "Have you ever visited Yei?"

Asha confesses she has not, even though it is less than fifty miles from her childhood home in Kajo Keji; the road was too bad to use most of the time.

"Everything was there!" says Lilian. "We had a house, chickens, trees full of birds. Everything was green and growing."

Asha sighs. Her life has been hard, always hard, but compared to this, it had also been good. She licks the dust from her lips.

"We had a nice house too when we went to Juba," says Asha. She is not boasting, just remembering. "It was a solid house with an iron roof. Three rooms."

The women are silent for a while. Lilian bites the cuticle of her little finger. Life goes on around them. Women sway past, balancing huge yellow jerrycans on their heads. The *boda-boda* boys chat under a tree. A little girl in a pinafore ripped down one side and knotted over a shoulder, plays in the dust near the cars, seemingly unattended. The wind is getting up; it's going to rain.

"See how we are," Asha says.

CHAPTER 25

Veronica

October 2017

A few weeks into the rainy season, Veronica gave birth at the health centre. The birth was fairly straightforward – she had grown since the last time, her hips more able to bear the pregnancy. She named her son Sadiq Jackson, after both the aid worker who was kind to her, and the baby's father. A nurse at the clinic questioned her choice of name: "Don't you know it's a Muslim name?" she'd asked. Veronica didn't know that, but neither did she care. She'd liked that name as soon as she had heard it. She fell easily back into breastfeeding and baby care, it all came naturally to her now. Her thoughts of Jackson, so acute during the pregnancy, began to ease off. She still had moments when she could not stop her tears. But over time, those moments became less frequent and lighter. She was not yet eighteen; she was still trying to take in what had happened to her in her short life and make a plan for the future. Her preoccupation now was to finish school. She talked to Wilbur about it and he had proudly showed her his primary and secondary leaving certificates – prioritised as essentials when he fled from South Sudan. She held the slightly dog-eared papers and examined their stamps of authority with reverence. Wilbur studied English, mathematics, commerce, science, geography, agricultural principles and practice, religious studies and history. How much he must know!

Veronica walks across the windy camp through newly planted vegetable plots to the primary school. A plastic bag dances in a gusty wind. There would be more litter in the settlement if there was anything to discard. She reaches Ofonzi Primary School in Zone One, a brand-new, concrete block built around a courtyard and painted in salmon pink. No one is guarding the gate so she walks straight into the open yard and to the first classroom on the right, peering through its glassless window. About forty students are inside, their exercise books open on rows of wooden desks. The youngest looks about ten, but the older ones could be older than her. She hangs back with her cheek against the wall so she can see in but not be seen.

The teacher, with a loud, clear voice, is taking the children through some points he has written up on the blackboard under the title "Uses of Plants". He reads each one aloud for the students to repeat. The first is source of food, followed by used for construction, source of medicine, provides fuel. If she was asked, Veronica could come up with an answer of her own. How about making furniture, she thinks, they haven't mentioned that. Her grandmother used to make cloth from tree bark – she could give that as an answer too. Just seeing a classroom at work again gives her a thrill. Although she had struggled in Juba she is determined to give school another try.

She crosses the courtyard to the school office. *Friendship Is Not About Sex* proclaims a sign with a UNHCR logo. *I Am A Girl, Do Not Make Me A Mother* reads another. A familiar feeling of shame pulls at Veronica, but she keeps on walking towards the wood-and-tarpaulin structure in the middle of the yard. She feels her heart thumping and stops to do the breathing exercise that James taught her. Breathe in, deep into the lungs, out slowly through the mouth. Three times. She steps through the entrance. It's dark inside, crammed with wooden tables piled up with mouldering exercise books, lever-arch folders and boxes of chalk. Two women sit behind desks. One wears a green silk blouse with her hair hidden under a pale yellow turban. The other is dressed in a tight, black satiny ruffle dress, with an elaborate hairpiece sitting a little too far back on her head. It is stifling in the room.

"Can we help you?" asks the woman in green, with little enthusiasm.

"My name is Veronica Joseph. I have come to enrol."

Both women eye her up. "What level did you pass in South Sudan?"

"P3," says Veronica, casting her eyes down to the floor. It was not an impressive level.

"Why are you so behind, child?" inquires the other woman, opening an A4 ledger marked "registration". She begins flicking through the pages. Her nails are long and painted gold.

"The war got us," Veronica says. "It got us in Juba. I came here by myself." She looks up, bravely. "With my child."

The woman in green raises an eyebrow.

"And now, I have another baby too," Veronica pushes on. "He is nearly six months, still feeding with me. I would like to know if I can bring him to class. My daughter can wait outside. She is a good girl, a quiet girl."

The woman in black looks up from the register and contemplates Veronica with curiosity and what Veronica takes for mild distaste. Small and neat, with luminous eyes and a shaven head, Veronica does not look to anyone like she could be a mother of two.

"You cannot bring your children," says the woman, firmly but not unkindly. "It is too disruptive. There is a place in P4 for next term. If you find someone to take care of them you can start then. You will need a uniform and some money for books."

Veronica feels faint. Part of her is elated. She is not used to being treated like an ordinary person making a reasonable request. She is much more familiar with being chastised or dismissed. She sits down to write down her name, her ration card number and her settlement address. She has hardly held a pen since she left Juba. She grips it tightly; her writing is slow and laboured; she does not want to make a mistake in front of these ladies. Who will look after Sunday and Sadiq? She tries not to think about it.

CHAPTER 26

Asha

November 2017

Asha's first child was born under the cloud of his conception. Asha was raped by the baby's father when she was seventeen and still at school in Juba. When her parents saw she was pregnant they sat her down and made her tell them how it had happened. Asha explained, and they marched her to the boy's house. They found him at home and called the police. The police came, but they were not interested in a prosecution; the boy was in Senior Six, just about to take his final examinations, and that kind of attention would spoil his future. The best thing, they said, would be for the parents to sort things out among themselves. And they did. The boy's family agreed that he would marry Asha, and in return her family promised that no charges would be brought. Such a pact was not uncommon and so began Asha's married life; her son Dumo was born a few months later.

With her mother's help, she was able to finish school. She was an excellent student and completed Senior Four the following year with four O levels. Life wasn't that bad, especially looking back on it. Asha's husband trained to teach English and chemistry. Although he only had a high school education himself, he soon got a job teaching students just a few years his junior. The rape was never mentioned again. There were no police records of any wrongdoing; his reputation was untarnished. Asha remembered, of course; as much as she tried to expel all thoughts of that day, the events were seared into her mind.

In the camp, after they had become friends, Asha explained to Lilian in a coded way about how she met her husband. Lilian understood. She was tactful. She was trained in the language of sexual violence, but she knew it would not be appropriate to use that vocabulary now. Asha explained that despite the way their relationship began, her husband had become very caring, and Lilian accepted that. When Asha's husband made an unexpected visit to the settlement, Asha introduced him to Lilian and Lilian greeted him warmly. He hadn't been able to bring anything from South Sudan – these days a South Sudanese pound could not buy a single maize kernel in Uganda – but Asha had seemed pleased to have him around and Dumo loved playing with his father. By the time he left to return to Juba, Asha was pregnant again. He needed to go back home to make some money, he told her. He had made no promises but, to Dumo's delight and Asha's quiet satisfaction, he returned before the end of the year, in time for the birth.

"It's time," Asha says.

Her husband is sitting on the log bench outside the house. Asha has continued to carry out her daily chores right into her ninth month of pregnancy and has just returned from fetching water. They are not a couple who waste words and her husband doesn't say anything now, he merely stands up to indicate he is ready to go. Asha picks up the small bag she has packed with the two sanitary pads she has been saving for the bleeding after the birth and a soft, cotton wrap for the new baby. She walks over to the liquor drinkers who have congregated under the tree and tells them there will be no service today, then goes to Lilian's house to ask her to look after Dumo when he returns from school.

It is a warm, pleasant day, and husband and wife walk slowly along the tracks that weave through the camp's modest dwellings. They are heading for the maternity clinic, where Asha is registered, a walk of about three miles. The couple stop frequently on the way, either for one of Asha's contractions to pass or to check the route – in Bidi Bidi's sparse, repetitive landscape it is easy to become disoriented.

Alosi Joy, a boy, is born just before midnight. The midwife notes nothing exceptional. The baby is small – not much over two kilos – a little unusual for a full-term pregnancy but perhaps that is to be expected as food has been scarce and the mother is away from home. Asha endures the birth almost silently; she is always reluctant to make a fuss. But she finds it excruciatingly painful, much more so than for Dumo's birth. The pain drains all of her energy, and at the end she barely has the strength to push. She is too exhausted to speak when the midwife places the wrinkled baby on her chest. She feels his tiny heart racing through his papery skin and sees the pulse on top of his soft, hairless head working fast. She breathes in his sweet smell and holds out her little finger for him to grasp. When the midwife is satisfied everything is in order, she sends Asha's husband home and leaves the new mother in the delivery room to rest.

Asha sits, holding the baby, afraid to sleep. It's the early hours and she needs to use the toilet. She has nowhere to put the baby so she carries him out of the room, her legs wobbling beneath her. The clinic is dimly lit. She finds the midwife sleeping on a mattress by the reception desk, snoring softly. There are other new mothers in the clinic's one ward and Asha can hear one of the babies crying.

"Madam, madam," Asha whispers, crouching down, still holding the baby.

She gently touches the midwife's shoulder and the woman opens her eyes. She is frowning. "What?" she asks sharply. "What's wrong?"

"Nothing, madam," Asha replies. "But I need to go to the latrine and I don't know what to do with the baby."

"And that is why you have woken me?" the midwife asks, making no attempt to keep the volume of her voice down. "Use your head, woman! You can see there is an empty crib behind you."

Asha turns around, still holding her sleeping child. There is a clear plastic cot pushed up against a filing cabinet. In the darkness, Asha can't see if it is clean or not. With her hand cradling her baby's head she carefully lowers him on to the bare, hard plastic. Immediately, his eyes open and he lets out a cry. Asha looks at the midwife.

"Just go!" the midwife orders, nodding her head in the direction of the door.

Asha scampers out into the night, across the yard to the brick latrine in the corner of the compound. On her way back, as she rushes towards her baby's cries, her legs buckle beneath her and she finds herself sprawled on the ground, with grit in the palms of her hands and on her lips. She is a poor mother, she thinks. So weak. She gets up and stumbles back into the clinic to reclaim her child.

Asha is discharged to the care of her husband the next day and to the couple's great relief they do not have to pay for the clinic's services. An advantage of being in the settlement is that healthcare is free of charge. Asha complains of abdominal pain and is given a strip of paracetamol tablets to take home with her. When they walk back in the morning with the tiny infant in Asha's arms, everything is as usual. The drinkers have gathered under the tree and the little children who are too young for school are running around in the dust. But outside the locked door of their house are two food sacks – the bigger one containing maize flour, another filled with cowpeas. She looks over to Lilian's house and sees her friend smiling at her. Lilian has organised it all, of course. All the neighbours in her village cluster – UN-speak for the group of about a dozen houses around her – have donated food they dearly need for the new mother's welcome-home present.

For the first few days Asha is allowed a break from the

usual routine. Men do not carry water, either in the camp or back home. A girl of eight would be sent to stagger back with a weighty container balanced on her head while her fully grown brother would merely watch. That is the way it is. Men can't be seen cooking either, while even the back-breaking task of carrying big bundles of firewood, often for miles, is the preserve of women and girls. So it is Lilian, not Asha's husband, who takes over her chores. Asha is not a confident mother but loses herself in the milky blur of the early days with her newborn in a way she wasn't able to when Dumo was born.

Inside her cool, dim hut, she lies on the mattress, covered in a pale blue sheet, with Alosi in the crook of her arm, next to her breast. She drifts in and out of sleep with the baby. He is a good boy, and barely cries. Every evening Lilian arrives with a pot of water that she has boiled and allowed to cool. They bathe the baby, watching him blink furiously as they lower his tiny body into the plastic basin. Lilian holds him while Asha gently cups the warm water over his head, and then cleans his whole body, paying attention to the black stump of his umbilical cord.

"He is not strong," says Asha, frowning as she massages Alosi's spindly arm with her thumb. The baby's ribcage rises and falls with his fast breathing. Asha can see all the veins under his almost translucent skin.

"He's doing well," says Lilian reassuringly. "He's feeding well. Give him time, he will grow," she says as she lifts him out to be dried on the bed. She folds a cotton square into a triangle, lifts the baby gently by his legs, pulls the cloth beneath him and expertly ties it up as a nappy.

Asha is glad to have Lilian with her – she is so capable. They share a quiet bond now, Lilian is Asha's best friend in the camp, in fact her only real friend. She can't count her husband, the drinkers or the women in the cooperative as friends. Actually, if she thinks about it harder, Lilian is probably the first friend she has ever had. As a child, at school, she always stayed at a distance from the other children and her siblings, it just seemed easier that way. She could never join in their jokes. She didn't enjoy playing games. If she joined in she felt like she was acting, pretending to be someone else, and she didn't like that. She spent most of her life inside herself, on the edges of the world around her.

A slant of morning light pierces through the thatched roof onto Asha's face. Still half asleep, she stirs, pulls her nightdress to the side and the baby to her breast. His lips are warm but his cheeks are unmoving, he has no interest in sucking, even as a drop of milk falls from her nipple onto the sheet. Asha sits up, holding him, and kicks her husband awake with her right foot.

"Quick, open the door," she says, with unusually sharp urgency.

Her husband, sleeping on the bare floor, groans as he comes round, and Asha kicks him again.

"Open the door!" she pleads. "I need to see the baby."

He groans again, sits up and crawls to the door, unbolts it and pushes it open. He hooks up the curtain that hangs behind it as a dust barrier. Daylight illuminates the room and Asha inspects Alosi's face. He is six days old. His eyes are closed; even when she gently shakes him he does not open them. His chest is working hard, his heart is beating even faster. Asha puts her little finger on his palm and his fingers close feebly around it.

"He's not waking!" says Asha, tears of panic falling down her cheeks. Her husband sits next to her on the bed and takes the baby from her, pulling up his left eyebrow to make his eye open. No response. He pulls up the other eyebrow. The baby's eyes look blank and glassy, his breathing seems too fast.

"Let's go," her husband says, standing up with Alosi in his arms. He dips out of the door and Asha, still in her nightdress, steps into her sandals and follows him. A few people are emerging from their houses, but the camp is still quiet. Quickly, without words, they walk the three miles back to the clinic.

Alosi never opened his eyes again. He stopped breathing at 2.24 a.m. the next morning, in his mother's arms. The nurse came over when Asha screamed. She examined the baby, looked for his pulse, and wrote down the time of death in his notes. They would have to wait for morning, for the doctor to come, the nurse told them, for the papers to be signed. Asha sat up till dawn, her breasts hard with milk as her baby grew cold in her arms. She stared at his face the whole time, examining his mouth, nose, ears, every eyelash and crease; she wanted to remember everything. His lips started to lose colour. Alosi Joy lived for just seven days, from 22nd to 29th November, Wednesday to Wednesday. Shortly after 9 a.m. a doctor arrived. The baby's body was taken into the examination room and his parents were ordered to wait outside. Ten minutes later, a nurse brought him out, wrapped in a white shroud. She handed the body to Asha's husband and gave them a form that the doctor had signed. The couple walked home again, Asha's husband carrying the almost weightless body. The drinkers were under the tree. They looked up when they approached and Asha saw the shock in their eyes when they noticed the lifeless bundle in her husband's arms, the face covered.

Asha and her husband stepped into their house and bolted the door behind them. No one ever told them why their baby died.

Two weeks later, Asha tells her neighbours she would like them to come to her house at five o'clock. Her belly has contracted and her breasts have finally started to dry up. Alosi, wrapped in a white shroud, has been buried in a small wooden box under a tree on the edge of their area. A priest came from Yumbe and there was a simple ceremony with a prayer. Asha wore her black dress with the little flowers. Her feet were bare as she watched her husband shovel a few mounds of earth over the coffin. After that, he packed his bag and returned to Juba.

As her neighbours start gathering, Asha is stirring a large, steaming pot over the fire. She flinches as the hot smoke scorches her eyes, she turns her head away but keeps stirring. She drops in a palmful of precious, gritty salt and wipes her hands on the skirt of her dress. She has swept in front of her house and has laid out a big, blue UNHCR mat made of woven plastic.

The event has an odd formality.

"Please," she says to each new arrival, gesturing towards the mat. "Welcome, welcome. Please, sit."

When everyone is seated, she goes around the circle with a basin of water. Using a plastic beaker, her son Dumo scoops and gently pours the water over the hands of each guest around the edge of the mat. It is a quiet, expectant ritual. Lilian, sitting with the others, follows her friend with her eyes. When all hands are washed, Asha goes back to her cooking fire, takes the lids off two steel pots and begins serving generous portions of creamy cowpeas, stiff, white *posho* and stewed spinach into plastic bowls. Dumo hands them out. Asha prepares dishes for herself and her son and they sit down with the others. She bows her head and thanks the Lord for the food and quickly crosses herself.

"Please," she says. "Let us eat together."

One of her neighbours opens his mouth to object – this is too much – but Lilian shushes him. This is what Asha wants. Like a jilted bride returning her wedding gifts, she has cooked all the food her neighbours gave her when her baby was born.

They eat slowly, with their hands, in companionable silence as the birds gather in the tree above.

CHAPTER 27

Daniel

March 2018

Daniel is not used to receiving good news, so when he's told he has been selected to take part in a six-week residential course at an agricultural college he wonders if there has been a mistake. But the joining instructions arrive, via an education charity that works in the camp, and in late March he is on a bus to the college set in green, rolling hills on the other side of Arua.

He arrives in an earthly paradise. An order of Franciscan monks has carved a perfect working farm out of the lush countryside, just an hour's drive from the safari lodges of Murchison Falls game reserve. On sixty acres, they breed cows, goats, pigs and chickens, there are neat rows of cabbages and okra, an orchard, a fruit nursery, even beehives. The opening class is held under the generous shade of an ancient mango tree. As Brother Alex, an exuberant, hand-waving Ugandan monk, outlines everything they will learn in their time at the college, Daniel looks around at the other refugees selected for the course and sees they are equally stunned to be in this enclave of abundance, where the breezy air smells of the red earth and they are served three good meals a day.

The six weeks are a dream-like time for Daniel. As well as learning skills from poultry keeping to pig breeding, cassava cultivation to honey production, he forms new friendships that bridge ethnic divides – friendships which would not have been possible back home and were hard to form in the settlement where resentments and rivalries still simmered. On the first day, he sits next to a young man of a similar age who meets his smile with a purposefully blank look. While Daniel doesn't bear the traditional scarifications of a Dinka man — lines branded around the head in adolescent initiation rights – his height and narrow frame distinctively mark him as a Dinka. The young man sitting next to Daniel is shorter, stockier – an Equatorian, he thinks.

When Daniel introduces himself in his quiet, low voice, he sees the young man swallow hard.

"Luka," he replies, turning his head away.

"Did you arrive yesterday? I think I saw you on the bus." Daniel perseveres in his questioning, either failing to pick up on his neighbour's hostility or choosing to ignore it, and when the class is dismissed he falls into step with his neighbour on the way to the open-sided canteen where they collect trays and line up for their meals.

The two young men sit down together and Luka appears to relax. He starts to speak. He's the eldest of six. Their father died when they were small, and their mother struggled to provide for them. She started a business making liquor and selling it to soldiers, at first just around Yei, where they lived, and then she began following the platoons when they went on the move – to Malakal, Wau and Yambio. She was last heard of in the town of Aweil in Northern Bahr el-Ghazal, that's when she stopped sending money home. Luka dropped out of school and they all got by on his earnings from his motorbike taxi. But in 2016 the trouble started. It was a difficult time to be a young man. Both sides were targeting the *boda-boda* drivers like him – Riek's men and the Dinkas with the SPLA. They hassled him, intimidated him, once knocked him off his bike for a beating. *Why don't you join us?* both sides said. *Why aren't you with us?*

The Dinka were the army of occupation. Most were simply cattle herders, but Salva had mobilised them and given them guns. They patrolled the town, taking whatever they wanted. Luka's siblings slept but he stayed awake the whole night, he tells Daniel. He knew when it was time to leave. He sold some of their belongings, including their precious portable DVD player. He rented a truck and driver to take them to the border. Checkpoints and questions all the way. Every time they stopped they had to hand over money. Luka had dispersed the money amongst each of his siblings; they all had something stuffed in their underwear. Every time they stopped Luka handed over a few notes. *It's all we have*, he said each time.

Where are you going? Why are you going? the soldiers had asked. *Why don't you stay and fight with us? Are you with them?*

"I told them I was taking my brothers and sisters to the

border," Luka tells Daniel. "I had to pay bribes all the way. Now we're in the settlement, I just want them to finish school. I tell them we must always behave like people who are blessed, even though we're not."

Luka looks around the canteen at the other students. He leans in towards Daniel.

"I don't want anyone to look at us and think we are orphans."

Daniel nods, pushing *posho* round his plate with his hand to mop up the gravy. For some reason he feels almost tearful. He's never heard about the war like this, from the other side.

But this brother from another tribe thinks just like him, speaks just like him.

The students rise to cool, bright mornings with dew on the grass. They wash their faces at the row of sinks and head for morning devotion. They stand in a wide circle in front of the administration building, more than seventy of them. They come from different faiths and denominations – Brother Alex and the other monks dispense with doctrine and seem to have a knack of including everyone in their prayers and worship. Afterwards come notices from the elected heads of the newly-formed committees, for sport and games; health and welfare; music and entertainment; dormitory and toilet block cleaning. There will be a football game that evening, a rota for cleaning is on the noticeboard, a guitar group will meet tomorrow after study and there is a prayer meeting for Muslim students. After the notices are read, Brother Alex wishes them a good day and the students file off for a breakfast of porridge and chapatis and mugs of masala tea.

Days are spent studying soil management and animal husbandry, climate change and account keeping – theory in the outdoor classroom and practical training in the fields and sheds of the idyllic, model farm. Nearly everyone here has grown up on the land, with a deep and easy understanding of the practicalities of cultivation and livestock rearing and a vigilance about an increasingly unpredictable climate. The theory, too, comes effortlessly to students like Daniel, but for others, with just a few years of primary education, it is a challenge. Repetition and rote learning are engrained and Brother Alex tries to make it simpler for those who seem to be struggling.

"So, as we have seen, wise use of fertilizer will bring a better... a better, what?" questions Alex. He looks expectantly at his students.

Hands shoot into the air.

"Yes, Susan?" asks Brother Alex.

"Harvest!"

"Correct!"

Susan sits back in her plastic chair, satisfied. Her neighbour pats her arm.

"And a better harvest may give us the chance to sell some... what? Can anyone tell me?" Alex chooses an older man in the front row to answer.

"Surplus!" he answers confidently.

"That's right!" says Brother Alex. "That's right. Well done. You are all learning well."

On the last night they have a feast. Braised beef in gravy with peas, carrots, *sukuma* greens, rice and sweet potato.

Bottles of soda for everyone. The canteen is noisy – spoons clanking on plates, laughter, voices excited and louder than usual. Just six weeks ago, they all sat down for the first time, shy and circumspect. What an experience it has been. For the women, it's the first time since childhood that they've been liberated from endless daily chores. The men have been freed from duty, responsibility and the machismo of living in war. Running in the background is the dread of returning to the settlement. Susan's eight-year-old son has epilepsy and suffers up to a dozen convulsions a day. She couldn't afford to pay for the medicine he needs. She has left the boy with her mother; being away from them both she has sometimes wondered if it has all been a bad dream.

Simon has six children aged two-and-a-half to fifteen, they are always hungry, and crammed into overcrowded classrooms at school. That is real life. The farm is different, a kind of Utopia, where men and women who would be enemies back home toast each other with sticky bottles of orangeade, and pledge friendship for life. Brothers, sisters, all.

When Daniel returns to the settlement he is resolved to build a better future on the small patch of land that has been allocated to them. The family has been moved to Rhino Camp, nearer the river, where the soil is a little richer. Under an unforgiving sun, he tills the family's small, sloping plot by hand and plants the okra and spinach seeds that were handed out at the end of the course. He sows the crop just in time for the rains, and now they can expect a harvest of fresh vegetables in August and September. Health education posters in the camp's schools and clinics stress the importance of a varied diet to health. But everyone is living off maize and beans, and usually just one serving a day. Daniel wants to contribute something new, something positive, that will improve the family's wellbeing.

"It won't grow here," says Daniel's neighbour, who never has a good word to say. His mother, surveying the neat furrows of earth that Daniel has dug, says nothing. She has seen plenty of failed harvests before. But Daniel is optimistic. The okra and spinach will just be the start.

"So, do you know about goats?" says a man with grey flecks in his hair and a blackened front tooth. A few weeks later and Daniel is sitting with a farmer in a village just outside the camp. Daniel is the first young man in generations of his family stretching back beyond memory not to own livestock. In the culture of both the Dinka and the Nuer people, cattle are glorified and revered. Cows are status, currency and insurance. The more cows a man owns, the more he is admired. If he wants to marry, he needs to pay for his bride with cattle. But Daniel owns not a single, breathing animal.

"Not much," replies Daniel, gulping down the water offered to him by the man's wife. She nods when he thanks her, adjusts her headscarf and returns to her morning's sweeping.

There are three goats tethered to a post and two more standing motionless with their flanks pressed up against the cool clay of the couple's house. The lower half of the house is painted white, showing it belongs to Ugandans from the so-called 'host community'. After months or years in tents, most refugees in the camp have built themselves similar, square, mud-walled houses. But unlike the local residents, they don't bother to paint them, they have neither the motivation nor the money. Daniel looks at the goats. He is instantly drawn to the smallest and prettiest one in the herd, almost comically endearing with a black and white coat, floppy ears and a wet, brown nose that is sniffing in the nothingness of the dirt ground. He squats down to pet it and laughs when the goat bleats at him in what Daniel takes to be a greeting. It is a male goat, obviously still an infant.

"How old is this one?" Daniel asks.

"Eight weeks," the man replies quickly. In theory that is old enough to leave its mother, Daniel knows this from his college course, but he has no idea how to verify the animal's age or indeed what he should be looking for in a goat at all. The animal looks at him with deep brown eyes.

"How much is it?" he asks.

"A hundred and twenty thousand."

Daniel laughs again.

"That's twice as much as I have," he says, truthfully.

"Then why did you come to buy a goat? You Sudanese are not serious," the man says, shaking his head.

The owner crouches down and rubs the goat's ears and jaw with his thumb, revealing the animal's teeth.

"This is a good goat," he says.

Daniel trudges back home through the dust, carrying the goat against his chest and softly singing Dinka songs. The breeder took all the money he had but was so furious to sell the animal for such a pathetic sum that he'd snatched the plastic cup holding the water from Daniel's hand then roughly removed the rope that was around the goat's neck, muttering that he'd been robbed.

The goat, at first tense and alert and struggling to break free, relaxes a little and bounces along with Daniel's footsteps, eventually succumbing to sleep. Daniel breathes in its sweet, musky scent and strokes its silky coat with his cheek as he walks. It is the first animal he has ever owned.

CHAPTER 28

Lilian

April 2018

Lilian has broken plenty of promises to herself since she lost Harmony. She said she wouldn't eat again until she found him. That didn't last long. She thought she wouldn't laugh again, but somehow she has. She has vowed never to change her dress, but of course she has bought a new one. It just seemed practical. She hated breaking all the contracts she has made with herself and the promises she has made to Harmony. Going back on her word has revealed just how weak and undeserving she is, she once explained to James, in front of all the others at counselling.

"Don't think like that!" James retorted. "Let's break it down. Let's think about each thing separately. Why did you start to eat again?"

This was actually a question to the whole group, Lilian was not expected to answer.

Jane raised her hand.

"Yes, Jane?"

"To stay strong?"

"Yes!" James was delighted. "To stay strong! What use are you to your son if you are a skeleton? Just skin and bones? How will you be able to cook his porridge then? Help him to read? Wash his clothes?"

The other women nodded.

"You have to eat because you need to be strong for Harmony!" James concluded, looking urgently at Lilian to see if the message had been absorbed. They discussed her new dress, how it had been necessary to buy it, how no one can live in dirty clothes and how important it was to look as good as one can for one's self-esteem. They even discussed the laughter – since Lilian had raised the issue. She discovered that nearly everyone in the group made these vows – never to smile, to laugh or to feel joy again. Like her, they felt to do so would be to dishonour the loved ones they had lost, to make light of the pain they had suffered. It would show a lack of respect, both to the dead and to the terrible memories of what had happened to them, the survivors. They all felt shame when they laughed again, usually at something trivial – a silly joke in the line at food distribution, a child's funny remark. But it also made them feel good, human again, almost hopeful. James told them many times that they must not be ashamed to laugh and smile, even to feel happy. It did not diminish the significance of what had happened to them. They did not need to bury their bad feelings, he said. With help, they could bear their weight and carry them into the future.

*

Lilian learns to live by James' mantras. In time, she stops going to the Red Cross tent for news of Harmony. Months have passed and she is thinking of her future now, not her past. She sometimes feels like she is playing a part, but she finds it remarkable, if she follows James' advice, how effective it can be.

"I will not allow my past to poison my future!" This is one of his sayings. Lilian even says it to other people now she is working as a volunteer for the International Rescue Committee. The position comes with an orange visibility vest with the IRC logo, as well as a worksheet and timetable. She receives a small stipend – two hundred and fifty thousand Ugandan shillings a month; more than sixty dollars: a lot of money in the settlement.

Being back at work gives her the same pride and purpose that it always has. Hard work is her comfort zone; it is what she is good at. Her duties expand quickly once the Ugandan and Kenyan IRC staff realise how competent and effective she is. She starts with a door-to-door survey in her village cluster, identifying women who need help, who are experiencing what the NGOs call gender-based violence – meaning they are being beaten or raped by their husbands, family members or neighbours. Some women need urgent medical care, some need a social worker or counselling. Lilian has suffered as much as all of them, or worse, but she never thinks about it that way. She helps them to find the support they need, and if she can't she tries to offer it herself – looking after children so their mother can go to the clinic, sorting out missing ration cards, even sourcing contraceptive patches for women desperate not to get pregnant again.

Next, she starts to organise regular group discussions at the women's centre that IRC has established just a few hundred metres from her house. It isn't much, but there are woven plastic mats for the women to sit on and a few toys for the children to play with. It is light and bright and somewhere to go. Lilian sees the pile of sandals left by the women at the tent door grow higher each day. She has finished the ten-session programme with James. She isn't a qualified counsellor, but she tries to pass on the knowledge she has learned.

She sees women who haven't washed, who haven't been cooking or eating. They don't have the energy to send their children to school or even to dress them properly. They don't want to plant seeds. They complain of aches and pains, but the next time she sees them their symptoms have changed. Life to them is meaningless, useless. Lilian knows what is wrong. She sees the pain in their eyes that she has felt herself. She makes it her mission to make them feel better, first to expose their feelings as James did with her, then to hear their stories and find ways to help them move on. It is a process, she tells them, a process that she has been through too. She has lost her son, her only son, her world! But how would giving up help her or help him? If she can move forward, she tells them, so can they.

Her house is one room, neatly arranged. She has a pink plastic shelving unit she had bought in the market in Arua and brought back to the camp on the bus. She has the photograph of herself with Harmony that her mother gave her. She had three copies made on that same trip and put one print in a black shiny frame. She has a little shelf with a mirror where she keeps her toothbrush, a comb, her hairpieces, a few pretty hair clips and some hand cream in a yellow pot. Her broom hangs on a nail on the wall. She has bought a mattress and a bed frame, and a mosquito net she rolls up into the rafters during the day. Apart from the photograph, her most precious possession is fairly new, a gift from one of the women in her talking group. It is a *milaya* bedsheet, made of standard pale blue cotton, but embroidered with the most beautiful design of flowers and birds. She'd watched the woman bring it to the women's centre each day with the material pulled taut in a wooden sewing hoop. The woman had some threads too, just what she had managed to grab as she fled her home – brown, yellow and red – not the prettiest combination but her stitches were exquisite. Lilian admired the work in progress and praised the woman's skill. She herself has never been good with a needle.

On the day it was finished, the woman held it up to the group and everyone clapped. In all this, she had made something beautiful. The woman's smile was wide. She knew what she would do with the bedsheet. She stood up and approached Lilian, who was standing at the front in her orange vest. The woman bobbed a semi-curtsey and handed over the fruits of hours of careful stitching. *It's to say thank you*, she said. Lilian was stunned. She stared at the *milaya*, absorbing the care that had gone in to making it. She held it against her cheek to breathe in its smell. When she began to cry, so did the embroiderer and most of the women sitting on the floor. The babies quietened and the toddlers put down their toys and returned to their mothers' laps, thumbs in mouths. Lilian dismissed them early – she could not talk again that day.

At night, in her room, the mosquito net unfurled around her, Lilian is not the person the other women see. She is a widow and a bereaved mother, but she is also a young woman, still only twenty-six. She rarely thinks or talks about her husband these days – if she does allow herself glimpses of the past then she lies there and reconstructs Harmony's life, moment by moment. It's painful, but it's something she savours. Less often, she lets herself think about Samuel, her husband. It was a short marriage, but such a happy one.

Now, in Bidi Bidi, she is alone without either of them. After her husband died, she still had the physical comfort of her son. Now he is gone too – no one has touched her for months. She is still young but in public she carries herself like a respectable widow; she cultivates an aura of unavailability. Secretly, she wants to be desired again, to be admired by another man. There are few to choose from in the camp. Most of the good men have stayed behind to look after the land, or even to fight. The ones who are here are mostly boys or drunks. However much she chivvies up the other women and finds the answers to their problems, when she lies in her bed at night, and thinks of her own life, alone in this purgatory, she wonders why God has spared her.

CHAPTER 29

Veronica

May 2018

Veronica lifts the plastic basin to shoulder height and tips the dried maize expertly into the bucket at her feet. The dust and chaff billow in a cloudy haze around her and the chickens scamper up, pecking at the nuggets of corn that missed their target. She puts the empty basin down and lifts the bucket to repeat the process, ridding the grain of the gritty dust. She hinges forward and swiftly sifts through the beads of maize with her fingers, discarding bits of husk and little stones, the chickens still scouring the slim pickings. She works fast, and once done she lifts the basin to her head, scoops up Sadiq and marches up the hill and across the dirt road to a wooden shack. Sunday trots barefoot behind them, struggling to keep up. Veronica barely notices. The noise grows louder as they approach; if Sunday tried to complain her mother wouldn't hear anyway.

"Customer here!" Veronica yells above the deafening whirr and clunk of the machine. A muscular young man in boxer shorts, cloaked in sweat and a dusting of flour, takes the basin, pours the maize into a sack which he hangs on the scale strapped to the doorframe. The dial wobbles and settles. It is too loud to talk but the deal is understood – he will grind the maize and take out two big cups as payment. Sunday pushes herself up against the wooden slats of the mill-house wall and giggles as the juddering vibrations run through her small body. Sadiq's fearful cries are drowned out by the racket; his mouth is wide and tears roll down his cheeks. A minute later and the container is handed back through the doorway. A perfect mound of soft yellow flour. Another woman arrives and proffers her buckets of grain to the boy. Veronica sets her wailing baby on the ground, swings the container to her head, dips back down to pick him up and strides back to the house, her daughter trailing behind.

It's expensive to use the mill, but Veronica can't waste time pounding maize by hand. Sadiq is a year old and she's going back to school.

The rain has eased off in time for the first day of term. The settlement is rust red and emerald green and still has that fresh, earthy, after-the-rain smell. Because she couldn't take Sadiq to school, Veronica sat out the first semester of the year, waiting until he was eating a bit of solid food. She has devised a plan for childcare – it isn't ideal but it's the best she can do. Her sister Amani, now nearly twelve, will go to school in the morning while Veronica does the chores and prepares the porridge. At lunchtime – it is called that despite there being no lunch on offer – Amani will return home to look after the younger children, swapping with Veronica who will go for afternoon classes, having breastfed Sadiq to tide him over until the early evening. He'll probably be crying by the time she gets home again, but that is how it has to be.

It's nearly time. Amani should be back soon, and Veronica will walk up to the school and take her sister's place in Primary Four. She is eighteen now, and will almost certainly be the oldest. She goes up to the little mirror hung outside their door. She checks her hair, rubs imaginary dirt from her cheeks, licks her lips and checks her teeth. She turns her head to one side to consider her profile and straightens the string of little turquoise beads around her neck. She feels ashamed that she can't afford the school uniform – a yellow T-shirt and grey skirt – for either herself or her sister. The uniform policy is supposed to instil a sense of pride and belonging, but Veronica thinks it strange that the school authorities insist on it, given that they knew the refugees have to sell their food rations to buy it. Given the choice of being dressed correctly or eating properly, most students choose the former, but Veronica simply can't risk selling more of her food this month – her breasts are smaller and drier and Sadiq seems to be constantly hungry. She sometimes clasps his little ankle between her thumb and forefinger while he feeds and worries that he's losing weight.

"When are you going, Mama?" enquires Sunday, not used to seeing her mother in this state of nervous excitement. They have talked about this day for weeks.

"When Amani comes . . . Oh here she is!" She spots her younger sister walking alone over the brow of the little hill above their cluster of homes. Her classmates are staying in school for afternoon lessons.

"How was it?" Veronica asks, when the girl has unhurriedly descended the slope.

"Fine," Amani replies, without elaborating.

"What did they say about the uniform?"

"Nothing," the girl replies.

Veronica knows her sister is annoyed, giving up half a day of precious school to be stuck at home to play caregiver to the little ones. She pretends not to notice.

"Supper is on the fire," Veronica says. "Quick, give me the shoes."

Amani kicks off the plastic sandals she shares with her sister. Veronica slips her long, narrow feet into them. They are warm and sweaty, and her heels hang over the back. She wishes she has a schoolbag, or even some books and pencils to take with her, but she has nothing. The sun beats down and Veronica sets off for her first school day in more than three years.

Her teacher wears metal-rimmed glasses and a thick, brown jacket with shoulder pads. He has a permanent, puzzled frown. He looks kind, Veronica concludes. The teachers at the school are Ugandan and follow the Ugandan curriculum, which Wilbur told her was different to the system in South Sudan. The salary wasn't much, Wilbur said, but the teachers got their accommodation and food thrown in too.

The other pupils are already seated after the lunch break. The classroom's walls are painted a vivid, limey green and the windows are open to let the breeze through, but the light is a little dim. The floor is bare concrete. Veronica takes the empty seat near the back that she assumes her sister has vacated. She was nervous on the walk to school but now she feels calm, expectant. She pulls in her chair and runs her fingertips over the battered wooden desk, familiarising herself with her surroundings. The solid wood, the smooth varnish, it is all a novelty.

"Good afternoon! What is your name?"

Veronica looks up, startled. The teacher and forty curious young faces are staring at her.

She bolts to her feet. "Veronica," she says. "My name is Veronica Joseph."

"Where are you from?" the teacher asks.

"I'm coming from Juba," Veronica replies. "South Sudan."

"You are welcome here," the teacher says, with an odd rising inflection which makes his statement sound like a question. Veronica is momentarily confused.

"Thank you," she says eventually. She sits back down and the class turns back to the blackboard. The first lesson is mathematics – division. Veronica tries so hard to concentrate she barely breathes. The others are writing in exercise books, copying the sums down from the board, calculating the answers with their pencils. Veronica has to do the workings in her head. Amazingly, she manages to solve the first two, but then the longer numbers flummox her.

Next to her, an undersized boy, probably younger than Amani, wears a big, brand-new yellow school T-shirt. Blinking slowly through thick, long lashes, he observes Veronica and her empty desk and gently pushes his workbook towards her so she can see. Veronica notices the perfect half-moons of his clean, trimmed fingernails. The boy carries on working in pencil, his calculations in neat, square print, carrying small numbers, drawing lines, whittling down the possibilities until he comes to his answer. For someone so young and small he is very assured, Veronica thinks. When he writes he presses down so hard on the squared paper that little bits of lead splinter off the end of his pencil.

The teacher paces up the rows between desks, looking down at the children's answers. His eyebrows are permanently raised, he is nodding, making a droning noise in his throat, *hmmmm, hmmmm*, but doesn't seem to be aware of it. He stops between Veronica and the boy. *Please don't say anything*, Veronica thinks.

"Don't you have a book, some paper?" The teacher tilts his head to the side and frowns slightly. He still looks quizzical, not angry.

"No, sir," says Veronica. "I . . ." She doesn't know what to say. She can't promise to bring an exercise book tomorrow, or next week, she doesn't have one.

"Er, we are working together, sir," the little boy says quickly. Under his lashes, his eyes dart sideways to Veronica.

"Hmmmm, very good," the teacher nods, and paces back up to the front and picks up a piece of chalk.

"All finished?" he asks. "Who will give me the answer to question one?"

Hands shoot up, including the boy's, his shoulder strained and his fingers splayed in an effort to get the teacher's attention.

Veronica gazes at him. It's her first day at school and she feels like she's made a friend already.

*

When the bell rings for the end of the school day, she sits still with her hands holding the sides of her desk as chairs scrape around her and the children file out, laughing and pushing. Some have black backpacks with zips and pockets. Her neighbour stands up and hesitates for a moment, perhaps wondering if he should strike up a conversation with this new girl, woman even, years his senior, or go off with his friends. He looks even smaller standing; his big T-shirt cover his shorts so it looks like a dress. Veronica smiles and nods slightly as if to dismiss him, and he scampers gratefully towards the door and his friends. The teacher has wiped the sums off the board and has started writing up the lesson for the morning. The Rivers of Uganda. He underlines it firmly with a stub of chalk.

Veronica heads noiselessly towards the door.

The teacher turns to her. "Did you enjoy your first day?" He still looks startled behind his glasses.

"Oh, yes, thank you, sir." She continues towards the exit.

"That's good. We are glad to have you here. But *hmmmm*, you know, if you miss half of every day you will struggle to pass this grade." He eases open the ill-fitting drawer of his teacher's desk and takes out two yellow-backed exercise books and a pencil.

"*Hmmmm*, here," he says, handing her the stationery. "If you write down the next day's work before you leave, you'll have a chance."

Veronica stays for an extra half hour while her new teacher patiently explains the whole of the next morning's lesson.

She thanks him, many times, and leaves the classroom, clutching her precious books to her chest. She skips home, chatter whirring in her head. She's telling someone about her day – Jackson, of course. She has tried to jettison him from her thoughts, but who else would she talk to about this? The big things – her father's death, the war, her mother – she has her counselling for that. It isn't that, it's the little things. Like all the things that happened to her on her first day of school. What the teacher said, what the kids were like, what she learned, the things she didn't understand. She doesn't have anyone to talk to about that. All the way home she chats to Jackson, her limbs light. He always listened. He was always patient.

She can hear his voice in her head. Gentle, with the hint of a smile.

Well done, Veronica. I am proud of you.

She is nearly home. Smoke drifts around the camp as residents start their supper fires. She reaches the top of the low rise that descends to her house and hears her baby wailing.

CHAPTER 30

Daniel

June 2018

The World Cup brings some much-needed excitement to the settlement. The favourite teams among the refugees are Brazil, Egypt and Nigeria. Some of the more business-minded residents have borrowed money and have bought big screens and DSTV connections for the tournament, screening matches in bamboo-walled video halls with wooden benches and little ventilation.

One Sunday evening, nearly three hundred men have crammed into a video hall to watch Brazil play Switzerland. There are more spectators than seats – those who have arrived early are perched on wooden benches but the latecomers have to stand at the back and fill space down the sides. By half-time, when Brazil are winning one–nil, it seems like all the oxygen has been sucked out of the hall. The spectators step out for some air, mopping their brows with flannels or

T-shirt sleeves. A few vendors are waiting with crates of bottled sodas but sales are thin; not many can afford it. After a short breather, the men jostle to get back inside – that's when the trouble begins. One man returns to his spot to find another man in his seat. The unfortunate thing is that the man is a Dinka, and the imposter a Nuer. The Dinka man asks him to move, the Nuer man refuses and a quarrel ensues just as the referee in Rostov-on-Don blows the whistle to kick off the second half. The Dinka man is bigger and he has his brothers with him. The Nuer also has some support – a group of his tribesmen who have been quietly resentful of having to share their home with Dinka refugees – people they see as aggressors in South Sudan's war. The two sides trade insults, then fists are thrown and others begin to wrestle. Benches are upturned, and as Switzerland's Zuber heads in an equaliser, the owner of the TV screen pushes furiously to the front to switch off the power and protect his precious assets from the brawl.

The fans are ejected into the still-warm dusk, scuffing the ground in frustration, a rare couple of hours of entertainment spoiled. There is a half-hearted attempt to restart the fight outside, but soon everyone is walking back to their home in groups, the Dinka in one direction and the Nuer in another, hurling insults at each other over their shoulders, but without much enthusiasm. They are annoyed at missing the match. Things got overheated and it would all die down – this is a refugee camp, not a battlefield in South Sudan.

When his neighbours return, Daniel – who couldn't afford a ticket after buying his goat – is sitting outside in the semi-darkness.

"What happened?" he asks, surprised to see them so soon, hunched and subdued.

"They cut it. We didn't see the whole game," says one young man, depositing himself on the bench next to Daniel, his knees splayed apart. His T-shirt clings to his sweaty body. He drops his forehead to his hands.

"Power cut?" asks Daniel.

"No," the man replies. "It was . . . well . . . everyone was being stupid. At least you didn't waste your money."

"Stupid how? You mean fighting?" asks Daniel.

"Yeah, they were fighting. Some Nuer hotheads," the young man says, petting Daniel's goat distractedly.

The boy yawns, but it doesn't seem quite natural, as if he is trying hard to appear relaxed. "It was nothing, they were fighting over a seat. Things got a bit wild. Anyway it's over now."

Daniel's mother serves up some stodgy maize meal with a few boiled beans. They eat slowly off tin plates as the whirr of insects rises with the darkness. Evenings in the camp are deadly boring; after dark, even if they switch on their solar light, there is nothing to do. If he's in a good mood, Daniel sometimes gets out his guitar or he and his sister play draughts with coloured bottle tops. But usually they just go to bed early. However optimistic Daniel has tried to be, sometimes life's limitations weigh heavily.

He is deep in sleep when he hears the first battle cries and at first he thinks he's dreaming. The Nuers are coming, marching towards them, brandishing weapons, chanting. *Don't be silly, Daniel, this is the camp.* His eyes are still closed.

He turns over, his bony hip hard against the thin mattress.

We don't say sorry to Dinkas and we are not sorry!

He hears it again. Louder. Has he really heard it? Sleep still pulls at him.

We don't say sorry to Dinkas and we are not sorry!

In Nuer, it has a rhythm. It isn't Daniel's language but he understands. He hears it clearly now. He sits up, stands up, stumbles around in his boxer shorts.

"Mama! Tabitha! Boys!" An urgent whisper. "Wake up!"

He hears the neighbouring huts start to stir, confused voices and a baby crying. What's happening? Who's coming?

We don't say sorry to Dinkas and we are not sorry!

In the darkness, Daniel fumbles under the bed that his mother and sister share. He is searching for the big stick.

The Nuer men have worked themselves up into a rage. They have armed themselves with pangas, sticks, homemade spears – anything they could find – and have advanced towards the Dinka areas of the camp. For them, the battle is unfinished. The Dinka men are caught off guard. They scramble from their beds, shout to the women and children to stay put, and, half-dressed, grab whatever they can in the dark.

It is raw, knuckle-splitting, hand-to-hand combat, amateurish in technique but deadly nonetheless. Before daybreak has brought a temporary, unspoken truce, two men are dead.

Later that morning, the police come from Arua. They park their vehicles up in a line, facing back up the road that will lead them out of the camp. The normally swept and ordered area around which the huts are arranged is littered with scraps of clothing, a single shoe, an iron ladle, an upturned oil drum and the plastic dishes that were stacked on the rack outside before bedtime. The brick kilns of the outdoor kitchens have been smashed up; there is a gaping hole in the grass roof of one of the huts as though someone has stamped on it until it fell through. The women and children remain indoors. The police find the Dinka men half-dressed, roaming, angry. The commander tries to calm them down, talking to them like children. *Now you are in Uganda. You cannot bring your fight here. You must be peaceful. Don't cause trouble!* But this man doesn't understand. The Dinka would not be placated. War has been declared, right here, in the settlement. They would avenge their dead. They circle menacingly, closing in on the policemen like angry footballers disputing a penalty, hands raised, fingers pointing. *Why are you here? Go and get the Nuer! They are the killers! Arrest them!*

For all the talk of brotherhood across borders, the commander looks into the red, bulging eyes of these men and sees strangers, aliens, hostile warriors that have nothing to do with him and his men. The police have guns and the refugees do not, but he fears an ambush, a battle, it will all be bloody. He orders his men to get back in their vehicles. The convoy speeds away, not to the Nuer side but straight down the road, out of the settlement. Those Sudanese, this is their battle.

The Dinka men cannot calm down. Living in the camp, with its rules and handouts, has made them impotent. They are far from their land and their cattle. Now they want revenge for the killing of their clansmen.

Daniel doesn't feel like that. He is a proud Dinka, but he's never felt like a warrior. He's never wanted to be a soldier like his father. One school holiday, two of his uncles on his mother's side took him on a hunting trip in the swampy wilds in Bor County. They taught him how to hold an AK-47, how to aim and fire. Some aspects of the trip he enjoyed – wading waist-high through rivers, sleeping out, the starry nights. He liked how his uncles spoke to him as an equal and they seemed to trust his abilities. They stalked gazelles and antelopes as eagles and kites circled above. Daniel was a hopeless shot and hated the deafening bang and the pain of the recoil into his shoulder. Most of all he hated the killing, cutting down a free, wild animal; it all seemed pointless and unfair. He didn't enjoy the trophy of the lifeless carcass, the blood or the gore. His uncles were perplexed. *So different from your father!* Daniel could only agree.

Now he stands outside his hut holding his only weapon, a wooden club. His little goat is bleating with hunger. It's getting dark and this disparate group of men, hundreds of miles from home, some Agar Dinka from the fertile lands around Rumbek, others Bor Dinka, like Daniel, have united around a common enemy. They spend the day singing the pulsing war songs sung by their fathers during the liberation struggle, dancing, pacing and laughing like hyenas to work each other up. They will wait until midnight and then head to the Nuer zone – there is no question: they have to take their revenge. Daniel feels sick. He has to do what is expected of him.

His mother emerges through the doorway. In the half-light, Daniel feels like he's in a dream. It feels unpredictable, dangerous. But his mother knows how it will play out. She has stayed inside all day with Tabitha and the boys: they have not cleared up last night's vandalism; they have not collected water; the fire is out.

"Stay here," she commands.

His mother is weary. How many times has she upped sticks and started again with nothing? Daniel doesn't know where she's got the money from. It's five days since the first bout of fighting, they have sold everything they can, and his mother and sister are sitting in the cab of a truck heading for the ferry crossing on the Nile. Each night since the football match, the fighting has continued, tit-for-tat. The Nuer came; the next night the Dinka took their revenge. There seems to be no end to the violent cycle; the Ugandan police have stayed away. Four young Dinka men have been killed already, and a dozen more wounded with pangas, sticks and spears. Daniel would be next, his mother said, there is nowhere to hide, we need to leave. They would take the ferry to the east side of the river, to Adjumani, where all the refugees are Dinka. They would be safe there.

Daniel is standing in the back, holding on to the metal side, his trembling goat at his feet. A hot wind blasts his face as the truck speeds recklessly through the interminable settlement, the driver's fist on the horn proclaiming their approach. Men wobble on bicycles, stiff-necked women halt in their tracks to steady the burdens on their heads, little girls guide toddlers to the side of the road. None seem to react to the storm of dust that flies from the truck's back wheels. They just wait, blink and continue their journeys.

Daniel sees they are approaching the river when the land

becomes green and lush. They have left the settlement but there was no boundary to say so. The Ugandan villages are nestled under wide, shady leaves, the houses are smarter, the children look plumper. The truck drives on, through the little town of Obongi to the jetty and joins the line of vehicles. The ferry pulls in, the ramp winched down and six vehicles rumble off, followed by foot passengers – women with baskets, men with hands in pockets. There are car horns and shouts as the return load starts to board – a swift, seamless operation that leaves Daniel's truck behind an ancient, blue-painted lorry spewing diesel fumes from its exhaust. The captain yells but the lorry driver indicates with a pained expression and a flurry of urgent gestures that he is too nervous to switch the engine off, he might not be able to revive it on the other bank.

Picking up his unhappy goat, Daniel climbs down from the truck, pops his head into the cab to see his mother and sister jammed in with two metal pots and food tied in plastic bags on their laps. They looked impassive but he sees the twitch of his mother's mouth. He walks between the lines of vehicles to the bow of the boat. The Nile spreads out around him and the air smells fresh and damp, like the summerhouse in Bor.

Water birds glide around an island of reeds and two men in a dug-out boat paddle softly away from the ferry. He closes his eyes and breathes again. Away from the tension of the camp, not just the violence and the hardship but that wheel of unmet hope, he can see it clearly now. He needs a new life.

CHAPTER 31

Lilian

July 2018

When Lilian wakes up she finds her heart is beating fast and she feels strangely restless. She owns three dresses these days – the yellow one, the one patterned with bright geometric shapes and the dreary brown dress from her mother. She chooses the yellow one. She goes about her morning chores and heads up to the women's tent. There is a savings club meeting today. They have started a small cooperative selling tomatoes, onions, sugar, salt, and silver fish from the Nile. Everyone who is able has put in a little bit of money, or has given time, or has walked long distances to carry the goods back from town. Lilian has kept a ledger of everything. By Christmas, everyone will be able to take out some money to buy some luxuries – shoes, laundry soap, underwear or a chicken. But then they will keep saving, because they have another goal in mind – to buy a sewing machine to start their own tailoring business. For that they will need four hundred thousand Ugandan shillings. The whole thing has been fun, choosing a name, assigning roles, sharing ideas. It has made them feel useful.

Lilian is standing outside the women's tent, chatting to one of the ladies, when a car pulls up. She doesn't really notice it at first, but when she looks she sees it is a big white Land Cruiser with a giant radio aerial bouncing on the front and the UN logo on the side. It isn't out of the ordinary – they have probably come to do a workshop or something like that. The driver keeps the engine running while a man and a woman climb out of the back seat, bid good morning to Lilian and her friend and remove their sandals to enter the tent. In the doorway there is some discussion and Lilian sees one of the women in the savings club gasp and put her hand to her mouth. Then she grabs the man by the elbow and marches him back outside, back towards Lilian. The other woman follows.

"These people are looking for you! They have come to find you!" Lilian's savings club friend exclaims. She is shaking the man's elbow; her eyes are shining. "They think they have found your son. They think they have found him!"

At first they sit in silence. Lilian says she doesn't want to know anything. She won't look at the file they have with information about the child. She has agreed to go with them in the car but she's certain she's going to be disappointed. She sits in the back seat and refuses to speak. The seats are black and cushioned and very comfortable. The UNHCR woman sits beside her; they have both followed the driver's instruction and buckled their seat belts. It's their policy, he said.

Lilian stares out of the window. In the comfort of the air conditioning, through the tinted glass, all the noise shut out, the settlement looks almost quaint – thatched roofs, children playing, women swaying with firewood bundles on their head. The car purrs, driven smoothly around the potholes; she is elevated off the ground, like a queen being carried in a litter. They drive out, through the villages, along the red dirt track lined with vivid green mango trees. A chicken runs into the road ahead, stops and freezes. The driver keeps his course and the bird goes between the wheels. He checks his rear-view mirror, raising a hand in a half-hearted gesture of responsibility, and they speed on.

The UNHCR woman hands Lilian a small plastic bottle of water. She accepts it, sipping slowly as she is driven to her destiny.

The woman is speaking. "Lilian, before we get there, before you meet him, we have to tell you what we know about the boy."

Lilian continues to gaze out of the window, pretending she can't hear, or she isn't listening. They are on the edge of Yumbe, a crop of competing NGO signs are planted by the side of the road. Pedestrians and motorbikes give way as they approach, there is no need for the driver to honk, a vehicle like theirs commands respect. Lilian can hear the sound of someone humming; it must be her.

"Lilian, we need to tell you everything, what happened to the child," the woman says. She slips off the rubber band from a big, hard-backed notebook and opens it to a page marked with a yellow sticker. "We need to tell you about him. Is that all right? Lilian? Can you hear me?"

The boy had remembered everything clearly. The UN staff had never come across such a young child able to give such detailed testimony. His vocabulary was beyond his years. They interviewed him on June 18th, carefully, sensitively, according to their protocol. Often they couldn't get much sense out of children, especially the ones who had lost their parents. But this boy was different.

He remembered leaving their home very early in the morning and walking all day. He remembered his mother soothing him when he cried. He was wearing his new shorts and his striped T-shirt. His mother told him they were going to walk to Uganda. But after they stopped walking and before they'd had any supper, something terrible had happened.

There was a flash, so bright it burnt his eyes. And a bang, so loud it knocked him over. The world went black, and afterwards there were fires and smoke and everyone was screaming and crying. The boy had looked around for his mother, but the world looked different; he thought maybe he was dead.

The woman's notes told her that the interviewer asked the boy at this point if he wanted to carry on; the interviewer told the boy he didn't have to talk about anything that he didn't want to – anything that made him feel sad or frightened. The boy told them he wanted to continue, but they took a break of fifteen minutes first.

Lilian sits staring at the countryside as it passes the car window. Green fields, red-brick tobacco towers, breezy laundry on a line.

The boy couldn't find his mother. Perhaps she had been blown up to heaven, perhaps she'd run the other way. He wasn't sure. A woman took his hand and pulled him with her. They ran away, they ran and ran until they reached a water pump. His shoes were gone and so was his T-shirt. He remembered thinking his mother would be angry about that. He drank from a bucket and slept on the ground.

After that, the boy and the woman walked for many days. The UNHCR woman goes on. Lilian appears impassive. The car has turned on to the smooth tarmac, it moves effortlessly; Lilian feels like she is floating.

The woman is still talking. The walk was hard. The boy and his new guardian walked alone for many days and barely ate along the way. One day, they passed a house, and an old man gave them some pumpkin to eat. On the other days there was nothing. The boy had to walk without shoes and there was blood on his feet. Sometimes the woman carried him, but one time she tried that and they both fell to the ground. They stayed off the road because they were afraid of soldiers. They slept under trees, without a cover, and although the woman was kind, at night the boy cried for his mother.

A tear escapes Lilian's eye. She feels it run down to her neck.

The woman turns the page. The two men in the front seats discuss directions.

"Shall I carry on?" the woman asks.

Lilian sits very still. A vein throbs in the side of her forehead. She raises her chin, almost imperceptibly, to signal her assent.

There was a record of the pair crossing the border to Uganda at Kaya and registering as refugees on October 6th, 2016. The boy was one of tens of thousands of children who had been separated from their parents in the chaos of war. It was common for these unaccompanied minors to be fostered into new family groups by older siblings, aunts, distant relatives or even strangers. Lilian knows this. At the registration centre, the woman requested a transfer to Rhino Camp, south of Bidi Bidi, past Arua. She believed she had relatives there. A pink ration card had been issued for the boy and his new foster mother on October 10th. The boy was enrolled in school, and according to the register had started classes at the start of the new term in February 2017. His reports were excellent.

"We believe that lady cared for the boy very well," the woman says, scanning Lilian's face for a reaction. "And the teachers say he is a very clever boy, he's already been promoted to P3."

A few weeks ago, the boy's foster mother had fallen sick, the UNHCR official continues. She was feverish, she lost weight. She was taken to the clinic in Rhino Camp. The boy was found trying to light the fire by himself. He was taken in by some neighbours but they could not keep him. The neighbours informed the school and the school informed the Red Cross. They questioned him carefully, and they asked him if he could remember anything, anything about any relatives or people who might know him in Uganda. They asked him to think very hard. That's when he recalled the information about his grandmother, in Koboko. He even knew her name.

"They tracked down the grandmother and she explained that you, Lilian, are the child's mother. She knew you had gone to Bidi Bidi. That's how we found you," the woman says, looking directly at Lilian, who refuses to meet her gaze. "Two years is a long time for a child of his age to be away from his mother. But I think he will be happy to see you."

Lilian lets out a sob – an anguished, howling sob – then she cries, wails, her face contorted. What is happening? She lurches forward; the seatbelt locks and holds her back. The woman puts a calming hand on her knee.

Lilian cannot believe this, she cannot. After all this time? It cannot be true.

At the roundabout the tarmac stops and the car bumps on to the dirt road to Koboko – the same road Lilian walked along nearly two years ago as a dirty, destitute and childless refugee. There is a low rumble in the sky. Lilian counts slowly in her head. One, two, three. She is only at six when the gush of tropical rain ambushes the car, big drops drumming hard on the roof, a curtain of grey quickly obscuring the world around her. The driver slows the car to a crawl and leans into the windscreen as the wipers flick frantically back and forth. Lilian has stopped crying. She wipes her nose on her forearm and rubs her eyes with her fists. Her mouth tastes sour.

The woman has stopped speaking. The man in the passenger seat is checking something on his phone and giving instructions to the driver. Lilian is grateful for the rain. The car feels like a cocoon. They could be anywhere, on any day. Those things the woman said to her, maybe it hadn't happened? Maybe she just heard it all in her head? Lilian stares at the woman, hungrily examining her, as if she would discover something. The woman stares back, vaguely alarmed. She doesn't try to touch Lilian again. She leans forward and mumbles something to the man in the passenger seat, her cheek against the headrest of the front-seat. The man turns around to look at Lilian. He smiles a little, and nods, as if to reassure her.

"So, Lilian, we are just arriving in Koboko. We're going to be looking for your mother's house. Do you know where it is?" the man asks, a little too loudly. Lilian looks out at the grey fog of rain outside the window. They have just turned into the main street; she can make out figures moving quickly, shopkeepers dragging crates, dry goods and bicycles under blue tarp awnings. The car's headlights are on, illuminating the muddy wet path; the smell of the wet earth wafts through the air conditioning. She looks back blankly at the man. She does not answer his question. She does not want this responsibility. She does not want to be part of this useless mission. She turns back to the window and looks up through the wet haze. She can see the red light blinking at the top of the giant telephone mast.

Lilian has her bearings now. They slow to a stop at the next crossroads and a vehicle behind them honks. Its lights glare through the back window. But their driver doesn't know which way to turn. Left, Lilian thinks, but she doesn't say it out loud. The driver turns the wheel clockwise; *it's the wrong way,* thinks Lilian. The rain is easing, falling in gentler slants; the driver slows the wipers. The view clears and they drive past the petrol station, past the church; they are on the Kaya Highway towards the border. *It's the wrong way*, thinks

Lilian, her mother lives behind them, back there, they are driving away from her house. She closes her eyes and drops her shoulders, easing back into the soft seat. They will have to work it out.

The car goes on, then stops, turns and stops again. The driver opens the electric window with a smooth buzz and Lilian feels the warm, humid air on her face. She hears him ask something in Lugbara. She hears a man respond – his voice is high-pitched, rapid fire. Her eyes are still closed but she can tell he is moving his hands. She scrunches up her eyelids. She does not want to see. She resists the urge to help. The window whirs up and squelches into its rubber seal. The car drives on, still slowly, the driver is still unsure, turning this way and then that. Lilian tries to zone out, meditate, keep her eyes closed, pretend she isn't there. *It's not my business,* she thinks.

The car stops. The others confer. Seat belts unclick. Doors open. Lilian's door. She senses the light through her eyelids and smells wet ash and cow dung. She sniffs; her nose is still wet from crying.

"Lilian?"

It's the woman.

"We're here. Take off your seat belt."

Lilian fumbles with her right hand and releases the belt. She opens her eyes. White specks obscure her vision, like burning dots on a film reel. She blinks, coming round. She absorbs the woman's face. The driver is there and takes her arm to help her down from the car. She steps carefully on to the soft, wet ground. She is standing and the driver is still holding her arm. She looks ahead, they are outside a square, brick house. Rainwater drips from the thatched eaves.

Her eyes track down. She sees a face and her brain computes. That face, her mother's face. But it is somehow different, softer. Why is she smiling like that? It doesn't make sense. Lilian follows the line of her mother's arm, held out to the side, around something. Lilian has to force herself. Her eyes move down, inch by inch. A child's head. Hair shaved close.

The world falls away.

Her hands are on his face, her forehead against his, her tears falling on his skin. She inhales his smell, like salt and honey, her fingers run over his smooth cheeks to the soft flesh of his earlobes. She pulls back to look at him, to be sure. Charcoal rims around his eyes, a scar on his eyebrow, a missing front tooth, pink gums. Harmony is smiling.

Lilian falls to her knees; the yellow cotton of her dress sinks into mud. She steals another look at the child and yelps and laughs with wonder. She drops her head. With her hands laid on her son's belly like a healer's, she starts to pray.

EPILOGUE

When I finally visited South Sudan's capital, Juba, the city was being scrubbed up for a celebration. Under the watch of armed police, work-gangs of barefoot prisoners in orange cotton uniforms swept the streets and repainted the black-and-white stripes that smartened up the kerbstones. The South Sudan flag – a black, red and green tricolour with a blue triangle and yellow star, the symbol of the new nation – was hoisted along the main roads from the newly opened airport. Huge billboards featuring President Salva Kiir in his black cowboy hat warmly shaking hands with his gap-toothed rival Riek Machar proclaimed a new dawn of peace.

But scars from the violence that the new capital had witnessed during five years of civil war could not be erased. Bullet holes peppered the whitewashed walls of the presidential palace, which in more hopeful times had been adorned with the golden silhouettes of elephants with their trunks intertwined. A brand-new office block stood derelict, its smoked-glass exterior shattered into spiky, hazardous shards. Right in the city centre, tarmacked roads gave way abruptly to puddle-strewn dirt tracks, indicating where construction had suddenly ceased. And despite the fluttering flags and bullish posters – *Blessed are the peacemakers!* – a feeling of menace still percolated through the city. Outside a shop selling bottles of soda, packaged snacks and little bags of laundry soap, I watched – from the passenger seat of a taxi – a man being brutally beaten and kicked as he lay face down and motionless in the gutter. "Thief," my driver said dismissively, fiddling with the knobs of his ancient car radio.

On a baking hot day, celebrations to mark the signing of a new peace accord were held in Juba. A national holiday had been called, shops and businesses were shut and everyone was invited to celebrate a new era of peace for South Sudan. There had been several false dawns but this time it would be different, their leaders would have the people believe. Riek Machar flew in from exile in South Africa, setting foot in Juba for the first time since he fled under a hail of bullets in July 2016, when an earlier agreement collapsed. The leaders of neighbouring Uganda, Sudan and Ethiopia, whose diplomats had helped to negotiate the latest deal, also came to witness the ceremony at the parade ground in front of the mausoleum of South Sudan's independence hero, John Garang.

The instigators of a war that had cost an estimated 400,000 lives and forced a third of the population from their homes were uncharacteristically contrite: "I want to apologise on behalf of all the parties for what we have caused you, our people… I deeply regret the physical and psychological wounds you have suffered," said President Kiir. His deputy-turned-adversary Riek Machar asked for the people's forgiveness and promised that the war was over.

Sloping down from the grandstand where the dignitaries were giving speeches, a wide grassy park had been given over to the celebrations of civilians representing the country's many different ethnic groups and allegiances. Everyone had been given little South Sudan flags to wave. It wasn't a spontaneous gathering; the buses that had delivered them there were parked up in rows, ready to take them home again at the end of the day. A dance troupe of young women wearing beaded belts moved in a circle with subtle, expert movements of the hips and shoulders, arms bent at their sides. Another group danced exuberantly around a whirling young boy in white knee socks and long shorts. A man with a feathered headdress danced and yelled and waved his stick, while a group of girls in matching floral dresses stood in a line to sing.

I had joined the crowd in the morning, flashing my press card to soldiers on the gate and to other officials – real or apparently self-appointed – who queried my presence as a foreigner. Some people wanted to chat and pose for selfies and seemed genuinely hopeful of a new era of peace. But beneath the surface there was an undercurrent of mistrust and suspicion. As the sun blazed overhead, I made my way down to a tree offering some sparse shade in the bottom corner of the field. Women sold plastic bags of popcorn and bottled water, corn cobs were cooking on grills and young girls wove through the crowd with trays of bananas and peanuts.

Sitting on the ground against the tree trunk was an old man in a moss-green uniform. As I walked past he summoned me down to speak to him. He had milky eyes, wiry grey hair poked out from under his green cap, and the coarse fabric of his trousers hung from his bony knees. He was the only elderly person I had seen in Juba. He was a veteran, he told me; he had served for thirty-five years as a ranger in the Wildlife Service, armed with a rifle to try to protect the multitude of species that had roamed South Sudan from poachers and wayward soldiers. There had been elephants, lions, white rhino, leopards and giraffes, he said. I noticed a small group had gathered around us, monitoring our conversation. The old man had lived through the Second World War, then two more wars over four decades between the south and the north, followed by civil war in the new South Sudan.

"These people are thieves," he said, indicating to the politicians on the podium. The speeches were blasting out through a loudspeaker, too loud to hear clearly. "They will not stop fighting. They will not stop until they have stolen everything."

I took out my notebook to ask him more about his life.

"That's enough. Stop now. He doesn't know the answer."

I looked up. A young man stood above us, wearing a shirt and tie under a jacket with shoulder pads, his hair slick with oil.

"Who are you to be talking to us?" the old man replied, frowning, waving him away. He wanted to tell his life story from the beginning, from 1934, when he was born in Yambio,

Western Equatoria, amid the neglect of British colonial rule. But he had barely started when the young man hoicked me up by the sleeve of my T-shirt and marched me back up the field.

"Don't ask questions," he said.

The rumblings of scepticism I felt on that day were well founded. The complex personal and ethnic rivalries that characterised South Sudan's civil war meant a peace deal could never be simple. The war triggered by Kiir and Machar had exploded into a chaos of factions and militia groups, all battling for a share of what was left of the country's resources. A genuine ceasefire needed all of these fragmented groups to be reined in, and issues that had been set aside in the push to sign the deal needed to be resolved. Peace deals had collapsed before and after a few weeks of calm, fresh fighting broke out in Central Equatoria. The government of national unity mandated by the peace deal failed to materialise and, in the first six months after the agreement was signed, the UN reported that more than a hundred South Sudanese civilians had been killed by armed militia.

At the Juba celebration, President Kiir urged all refugees to return to their homeland – as if it was their patriotic duty. But across the border in Uganda, the residents of Bidi Bidi, still nursing the traumas that forced them there, weren't convinced. It was too soon to go back. Life in the camp continued as normal.

Lilian has a second son now, Godfrey. He's just started walking and I can hear him babbling in the background of our WhatsApp calls. She never felt the same love for Godfrey's father as she did for Samuel – or "Baba Harmony", as she calls him. While she was pregnant, Godfrey's father left the camp, set off for South Sudan and never came back. He worked as a medical technician and left behind sixty boxes of medicines, some of them out of date, which she tried to sell. With her small income from IRC, she had just saved enough money to send Harmony to a private school in Arua when she lost everything, again.

After she was reunited with Harmony, Lilian had thrown herself into the work she loved as an IRC outreach worker. She became known across her zone in Bidi Bidi as the go-to person for women who had problems – the ones with abusive partners, the ones who couldn't cope, the ones with suicidal thoughts, and the ones who needed contraception, medicine or help with school fees. Lilian would help anyone who asked.

In 2019 she became involved in the case of a woman who had been badly beaten by her husband and throttled in front of their children. It was only because one of the children ran from the house to get help from a neighbour that the attack had stopped. She reported the matter to her seniors at IRC who in turn took the case to the police. The woman's husband, a refugee like all of them, was detained, questioned and released pending further investigation. The police took a statement from Lilian. The man went straight back to his wife and beat her again, and that same night, when he was high on opium and Lilian was asleep with Harmony and the baby, he came to her home in Bidi Bidi and set a flaming torch to the thatched roof that she had just made good for the rainy season.

The smell of burning, dry grass woke her. She grabbed Godfrey in the darkness and pushed Harmony out of the door. The family stood with the neighbours, barefoot and stunned, as flames danced up the conical grass-thatch, then engulfed it in a sudden whoosh. It collapsed into the mud and straw walls, making the spectators jump back from the flying sparks.

"Everything inside was burned. Our clothes, the medicine that Godfrey's father left, my documents, the blankets I bought for the baby. I just thank God I'm alive," Lilian said. "That man wanted to kill me. They never caught him; he ran away that night, they think he ran back to South Sudan."

Lilian never returned to the cluster of homes where she lived with her friend Asha next door. IRC put her and the two boys in a safe house straight away, and a few months later she was allocated a new piece of land in different zone of Bidi Bidi to make another fresh start. I spoke to her a few weeks into the Covid-19 lockdown in April 2020. A ban on gatherings had closed the women's centres, the schools, the video halls and the churches. She was at home with Harmony and Godfrey. Twice a day, she strapped the baby to her back, queued for water and carried the jerrycan back home on her head. Once a week, she must do the same in search of firewood. As the pandemic ate into global resources and wrecked economies, refugees were being pushed further down the list of priorities. The UN's World Food Programme hadn't been able to raise enough funds to feed the refugees in Bidi Bidi. Lilian's rations had been cut by a third; it was the same for everyone.

"I'm trying to be a good mother to my children," she said. "When we get food I make sure they eat before me. I need to eat greens, but I can't afford it. I also need sugar for the baby's porridge. The markets are empty and if something is there the price is twice as high. I feel afraid. Not just me, all the mothers here feel like this."

What about going back to South Sudan? She paused. She often talked to Harmony about their life there before Samuel died, she said. "We like to think about it. That beautiful place. We had banana trees. All our dreams were there."

But Lilian had heard about fighting around Yei, her hometown, from newly arrived refugees who have fled across the border to Bidi Bidi. They described abandoned shops, derelict houses, roads littered with burnt-out cars. Did she have faith in the peace process?

"To our leaders it is just a game. One day they've signed a peace agreement and then the next day they've changed their mind," she said. "There are rebels in the bush hiding out. There is still a lot of fear stopping us from going home.'

Daniel had barely got to the end of a brief thank you speech when his fellow students stormed the stage, lifted him up and crowd surfed him back through the hall and out of the door, so the celebrations could begin on the grass outside.

It was 2019, a few weeks before Christmas. After a lightning campaign, Daniel had just been elected President of the Students' Guild of the Makland Institute of Business and Management in Kampala. The ballot count – carried out in front of the two final contenders, a panel of professors and hundreds of students – was decisive. Akuei Daniel Bol, from Bor, South Sudan, had become the first international student to claim the position, which would bring him a small allowance and immeasurable prestige.

He was almost a year into his studies for a diploma in Economics and Applied Statistics at one of Uganda's top business schools when a couple of his South Sudanese classmates encouraged him to run for guild president. Although he briefly dismissed the idea, he didn't take much persuading. He knew he'd be the underdog, but he also knew he could win. He was popular around campus, very sociable, so much so he had already been given a nickname.

"They called me 'the boyfriend'. I don't know why, it was just stupid, I guess. It was like whenever anything was happening, I was there, so I got that nickname and it stuck," he told me by instant message. "For the campaign it was useful, we could just use the nickname and people would say 'oh yeah, I know that guy'."

There were rallies and debates. Daniel quickly found his voice. *For Betterness We Stand!* was his campaign motto and he promised to tackle the students' problems of poor housing, the intermittent electricity supply in the women's dormitories, dirty latrines and a lack of books.

His mother sold their goat; an uncle was persuaded to pitch in. His father was out of contact again, in the wilds of Jonglei State, protecting Dinka lands from cattle raiders. Some of the better-off students helped with contributions and the South Sudanese students organised a fundraiser. By late November, two weeks before the election, he had built a fighting fund of 336,000 Ugandan shillings – about eighty dollars.

His campaign team spent some of the money on posters which went up on every tree and noticeboard around campus. Flyers were printed and handed out around university dorms and lecture theatres. But their best campaign weapon was Daniel himself. He was constantly out around campus, asking questions, listening to problems, suggesting solutions. He discovered he had a natural eloquence, an ease with people, he knew how to pitch himself in any given circumstance.

“I found that people could relate to me, I found it easy to talk. I was always approachable, whereas my opponent didn’t want to talk to anyone. He stayed hidden behind his team for the whole campaign.”

Sixteen students started off in the race, but nine of them dropped out as they failed to pick up support. The seven remaining were interviewed by a panel, including the Dean of Students, who whittled the contenders down to two. Daniel’s opponent was a doctor’s son and had spent big on his campaign, which included professional photos and a YouTube video. But when the returning officer came on stage to announce the final result at 9pm, Daniel – wearing a borrowed, grey suit a little too short on the legs and arms – had won by a landslide.

“I only had time to say a quick thank you to my team, when the students stormed the stage, lifted me up and carried me out on their shoulders,” he said. “They threw me up into the air. It was a little much, I didn’t think I deserved it. But I was happy. As long as I’m alive, that moment will never leave me.”

After crossing the river to escape the World Cup brawls in Rhino Camp, Daniel and his family had settled in another camp, on the east bank of the Nile, where most of their fellow refugees were Dinkas like them.

The terrain on that side was a little better, the soil was a little richer, and the plot they were given was bigger. His mother and sister Tabitha seemed satisfied with their new home and set about digging the ground. All of Daniel's freshly planted vegetables had been abandoned in Rhino Camp. This new place was marginally better, but Daniel could not shake off his lingering dissatisfaction with refugee life.

In late August 2018 he set off back to Juba. It was still too dangerous for his family, but maybe he, as a single man, could find a job and make some money to continue his education. When I met him there in October of that year, he had lost weight. His legs, while fully recovered, were stick-thin, his cheek bones jutting.

"I don't have much appetite these days," he told me. He hadn't found a job, he was living at the grace of his cousin. He was poor, almost destitute, anxious about what he should do next. But there was one bright spot in his life.

He showed me a picture on his phone. It was of a young woman, a Snapchat-enhanced picture that gave her smooth, glowing skin and kitten ears. Even through the filter, I could see that she was beautiful, with a collar of coloured beads around her neck. It was Daniel's new girlfriend, Becky.

The daughter of an SPLA general, Becky had been at the same school as Daniel in Arua, a couple of years below him and a friend of Tabitha's. He bumped into her again soon after arriving in Juba. They started dating almost straight away, but physically meeting was difficult. Becky could not be seen to have a boyfriend unless they had plans to marry, and for that, Daniel would need to pay a "bride price" and be able to keep her in comfort. So their courtship took place mainly by phone. One afternoon when I sat with Daniel in a riverside cafe, they had four long phone calls in the space of a couple of hours; Daniel talked softly to her in English as she described to him the next happening in her day.

"She says hi," he said, smiling, as he put the phone back down on the table.

Although in love, Daniel felt downhearted. He had failed to find any kind of work, he couldn't study, he had no money to send back to his family, or indeed feed himself properly. Then came another of what Daniel regarded as his life's miracles. The Ugandan embassy in Juba advertised a scholarship programme for South Sudanese students to study at Makland in Kampala. After two interviews, he was in, packed up his meagre belongings, kissed Becky goodbye and headed off by bus to start the first semester in January.

It could not have gone better: he spent hours in the library, pleased his tutors and got good grades. He spoke to Becky by WhatsApp several times a day. He was well liked around the campus and by the end of the year he'd been elected President of the Students' Guild. But like all of the triumphs in Daniel's life, then followed misfortune. In winning the election, he had made an enemy. His opponent, the well-off doctor's son, believed the position was rightfully his. He had spent nearly two million Ugandan shillings on the campaign – more than six times the budget of Daniel's team – and lost. A week after the vote, just before Christmas, Daniel left his room in the male dormitory to use the outdoor shower. Hired thugs of his rival were lying in wait:

they raided his room, ripped up his work, stole his clothes and his phone, then hacked into his social media accounts and deleted them.

I lost contact with Daniel for more than three months – his phone number didn't work; he disappeared online. I found him again after the Covid pandemic had struck. His college was closed, all the students had been turned out of their dorms. The international students had nowhere to stay; his last duties as Guild President were to help them get home before the borders shut, using up the last of his small allowance to help them with bus fares.

Over a long WhatsApp call, Daniel told me that the world he had built had collapsed again. His plans to finish his diploma that year had evaporated. He was stuck, waiting for transport to start up again so he could at least join his family in the camp, help his mother and sister with their small plot of land. What troubled him most was news from Juba. Becky's school had closed, making her presence as a single woman at home all the more conspicuous. While only twenty-two, she was under pressure to get married.

"As long as she is studying, she can remain unmarried," Daniel explained to me. "That is the only exception. Now she's at home she feels a lot of pressure. Even her younger sister is married. I can't marry her until I have graduated. I want to be able to provide for her, give her everything she needs. But she can't hold out for me."

Uganda introduced one of the strictest coronavirus lockdowns in Africa. The refugees in Bidi Bidi weren't given much information about Covid-19. It was a nebulous fear, just one more concern on top of all the others. Schools were closed. Teachers, humanitarian workers and mental health counsellors left the camp, except those working on water and sanitation supplies. When I spoke to Veronica, her knowledge of the virus was still vague, but she knew it had been rampant in the UK, where I was. "We've been praying for you," was the first thing she said. I was shocked. Veronica was recovering from her third bout of malaria since arriving in the camp. Out of all the lockdown hardship stories I heard, hers – sick with a fever, confined to her windowless home with the children – was the most difficult.

Veronica's neighbour Wilbur had been in touch with me months earlier to tell me that Veronica was pregnant for a third time. She gave birth to a baby boy, Emmanuel. Wilbur said the community had rallied round to look after the young family. When I called, it was sometimes hard to speak to Veronica directly. She had a habit of handing the phone over to others – always men – because they had reached a higher level of schooling. But in fact, her English was usually better than theirs. I asked her if the baby's name had any particular meaning. It was her grandfather's name, she said. I ask about Jackson, did she know where he is?

"I have heard that he is in Congo now. It is hard for us to have contact. I don't know if I will see him again."

Does she think about him?

"I do think about him. Because of our love and our love for our children."

I was glad to keep up with Veronica's news. Each phone call or WhatsApp message via Wilbur brought word of some new life event that made me marvel about how much she had packed into her twenty years. But there is no way to put a gloss on the hardship she has endured and continues to endure in the camp. She was pleased that I had taken an interest in her, but she understood well the contrast in our situations. I had spent time with her in Bidi Bidi, but could come and go at will, I could retreat to the safety of home when I wanted to. She could not. When I went to the camp for the last time to say goodbye, she didn't want to chat. We were in tears. "Just go," she said.

AFTERWORD

After this book was first published during the Covid lockdown in late 2020, I joined the online meetings of lots of book clubs that had chosen *The End of Where We Begin* as their group read. I was secretly surprised that they'd chosen a book that was clearly full of sad, traumatic and sometimes despairing content at a time of such fear and uncertainty. But I was also surprised by their reaction – the stories of Veronica, Daniel and Lilian had helped them to put their own pandemic hardships into perspective. Many said they felt uplifted by the spirit and courage of these three young people and saw their own lives and troubles through a new lens.

This was wonderful to hear and I was able to relay their feedback to Veronica, Daniel and Lilian – who were still curious as to why anyone would be interested at all. I was also happy that the three felt they had ownership of the book, in which I was essentially the ghostwriter of their stories. This is what I'd hoped for of course, but I'd been worried that they might feel differently. At the Kampala launch of the book, Daniel was interviewed by the Ugandan writer and poet Surumani Manzi while I appeared on a screen from London. Daniel was wearing his suit and tie; he looked smart but so thin – his cheekbones sharp and his cheeks hollow. This was Daniel in his element – lit by a ring-light for viewers on Facebook Live and a full house in the African Studies Bookstore. Holding up a copy of the book he said: 'This book inspires me. This is my life story. It reminds me of who I am and where I come from. It reminds me that at this point in life, I can do anything.' That's when I had to switch off my camera to hide my tears. I found it so overwhelming that we had both arrived at this moment, nearly three years after our first meeting on plastic chairs under the shade of a tree. Now the book was published and these stories were being read.

Keeping in touch with Veronica, Daniel and Lilian over the past few years has made me realise I could have written this book several times over. This isn't a novel; their lives didn't stop at the point at which we left them in the narrative. They have all moved on, and the drama and struggles continue. They have lost everything and they have built up their lives again from extremes that would have broken most people. Each of their stories still seems remarkable, even unbelievable. In these young lives, could all this have happened?

Lilian was widowed, lost her son, found him again, was deserted by her second husband, became the victim of an arson attack and has lost her home twice. She's still in Bidi

Bidi and her focus now is on her children, especially ensuring that Harmony – twelve years old and the brightest child in his class – can reach his potential.

Veronica, who became a mother just before her fifteenth birthday, has given birth to her three children either in a war zone or refugee camp. Somehow she keeps going. With UN food rations in Bidi Bidi now cut in half, Veronica, who is still only twenty-three, has taken her children back to Juba, a city not quite at peace, but her only option.

Daniel's extraordinary life story continues. He is single again; his girlfriend Becky was forced to marry a man her family deemed more suitable. Returning to the camp recently to visit his mother and sister, a midnight knock announced another girl on the doorstep, a stranger. He let her in, falling for a plan cooked up between his father and the girl's parents for the two young people to marry. "Her family is threatening to harm me if I don't accept their daughter as my wife," he wrote in a frantic text. Faced with a marriage he didn't want, Daniel ran away again, crossing swollen rivers first into hiding in the Ugandan city of Lira, and then back to South Sudan.

What's become clearer to me since I wrote this book is that every story told here represents an injustice, a violation of the human rights to which we all should be entitled. The stories of Daniel, Veronica and Lilian are not one-off vignettes, but part of a wider global picture of violence, displacement and inequality. In 2021, *The End of Where We Begin* won the Moore Prize, a literary award for excellence in human rights writing, from a shortlist of titles by some of the female journalists I most admire, including Barbara Demick and Gayle Tzemach Lemmon. I was staggered (and delighted) that this book's seemingly small, personal stories could resonate, and their importance be recognised.

The Russian invasion of Ukraine, the outbreak of civil war in Sudan and the Taliban takeover of Afghanistan have now created fresh cohorts of refugees, and every day asylum seekers try to cross the Mediterranean and the English Channel by boat in the hope of reaching sanctuary in Europe. Millions of people like Veronica, Daniel and Lilian are on the move across the planet, trying to escape poverty and despair created by conflict and climate disasters. I hope this new edition of the book can reach as many people as possible to give a better understanding that every refugee – in every camp, small boat, holding centre, temporary hotel room or host family – is simply someone like us, with their own story of loss, love and hope that deserves to be heard.

August 2023

Resources and Further Reading

The author will share the proceeds of this book with the Milaya Project, a non-profit organisation working with women's collectives in Bidi Bidi settlement, connecting them with customers for their embroidered *milayas*. You can read more about them at milayaproject.org or follow them on Instagram @milayaproject.

TPO Uganda is the only dedicated mental health organisation working in Bidi Bidi. Its staff are now helping refugees to cope with the psychological impact of the coronavirus pandemic. You can find out more about their work at tpoug.org.

Eve South Sudan is a grassroots organisation helping to improve the lives of women and girls in South Sudan with projects to counter sexual violence and promote girls' education, health and equality. Their website is evesouthsudan.org.

Other humanitarian organisations working to help refugees in Bidi Bidi are the UN refugee agency UNHCR, International Rescue Committee, Save the Children, World Vision and War Child Holland. You can support their work via their websites.

For further reading on South Sudan's recent history, politics and civil war:

South Sudan: The Untold Story, by Hilde F. Johnson (2016)

First Raise a Flag: How South Sudan Won the Longest War But Lost the Peace, by Peter Martell (2018)

The Struggle for South Sudan, Edited by Luka Biong Deng Kuol and Sarah Logan (2019)

A Rope from the Sky: The Making and Unmaking of the World's Newest State, by Zach Vertin (2018)

A Poisonous Thorn in Our Hearts, by James Copnall (2017)

Breaking Sudan: The Search for Peace, Jok Madut Jok (2017)

Acknowledgements

My sincere thanks go to Veronica, Daniel, Lilian, Asha, James, Wilbur and their families for entrusting me with their stories, their support in writing this book and their continued kindness.

In Uganda and South Sudan I am very grateful for the help of Patrick Onyango Mangen, James Oola and Godfrey Twesigye of TPO Uganda; AnneMarike Smiers of War Child Holland; Jess Wanless of the International Rescue Committee; Cephas Hamba of Save the Children; Philiam Adriko of World Vision; Brothers Charles, Tony and Alex at Adraa Agricultural College; journalists Denis Dumo and Christine Wani; Peace Abaru and everyone at the Premier Hotel, Yumbe; and UNHCR Uganda.

Thank you to the following friends and colleagues for championing *The End of Where We Begin*: Helen Bendon, Benjamin Black, Aoife Cassidy, Samantha Chesler, Tamsin Collison, Siobhan Dunn, Helen Fricker, Bjorn Gillsater, Clare

Gillsater, Sally Hayden, Kieran Guilbert, Lucy Harrold, Kirsteen Kamming, Zoe Leon, Henry Makiwa, Alice Meadows, Katy Migiro, Katie Nguyen, Stephen Powell, Jane Russell, David Stocker, Michela Wrong.

I'm very grateful to Simon Edge and everyone at Eye Books for publishing this new edition of the book. Thanks to Nell Wood designing the beautiful cover, Egill Bjarnason for the cover photograph, Clio Mitchell for typesetting and to Anthony Spratt and Clark Left for producing the map of South Sudan and Uganda.

Huge thanks to my editors Vicky Blunden, Justine Taylor and Adam Manolson for their insight, guidance and attention to detail.

Finally, very special thanks and love to the Russell and Collison families, especially Dan, Ruby and Mattie.